MW01445280

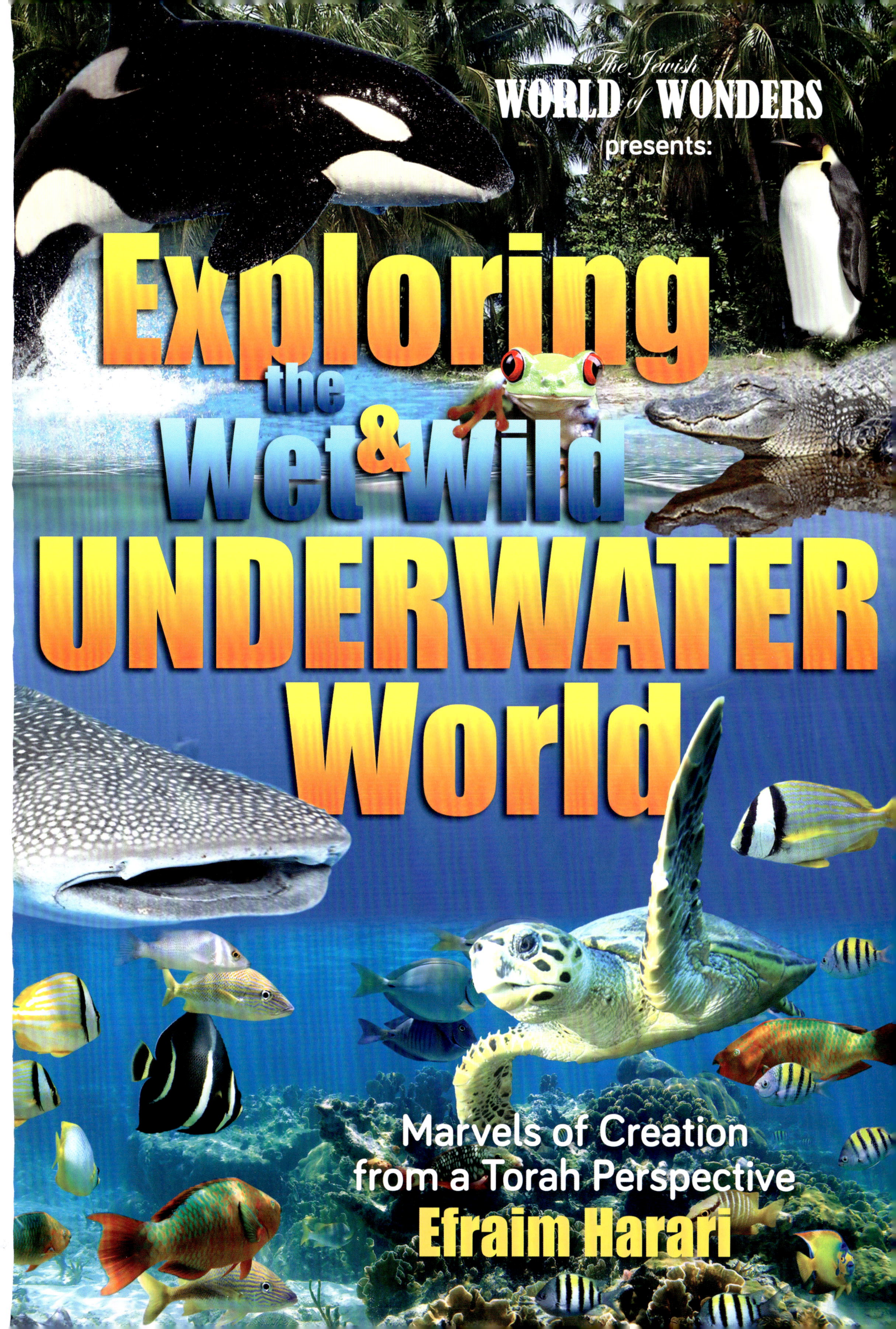
The Jewish
WORLD of WONDERS
presents:
Exploring the Wet & Wild UNDERWATER World
Marvels of Creation
from a Torah Perspective
Efraim Harari

ISBN 978-1-60091-233-7

Compiled and adapted by Efraim Harari
Book and cover design by Stacey Gindi
www.SGindiDesignStudio.com

Torah sources verified by Rabbi Michael Malka
Edited by Malkie Gendelman

Published by:
Israel Bookshop Publications
501 Prospect Street
Lakewood, NJ 08701

Tel: (732) 901-3009
Fax: (732) 901-4012
www.israelbookshoppublications.com
info@israelbookshoppublications.com

Printed in China

Distributed in Israel by:
Shanky's
Petach Tikva 16
Jerusalem
972-2-538-6936

Distributed in Australia by:
Gold's Book and Gift Company
3- 13 William Street
Balaclava 3183
613-9527-8775

Distributed in Europe by:
Lehmanns
Unit E Viking Industrial Park
Rolling Mill Road,
Jarrow , Tyne & Wear NE32 3DP
44-191-430-0333

Distributed in South Africa by:
Kollel Bookshop
Northfield Centre
17 Northfield Avenue
Glenhazel 2192
27-11-440-6679

Table of Contents

Acknowledgments

Even though my name alone appears on the cover of this book, by no means was this a one-man production. The creation of this project was only possible thanks to the creative and talented team of the people behind me. I would like to take this time (and space) to express my gratitude to the following people who, without their support, effort, and dedication, this book could not have been written.

The "first and foremost" person that I would like to thank is my wife. She has as much to do with the creation of this project as I do. Truth to be told, I rarely do anything by myself – my wife is always by my side, either physically or spiritually. I am truly blessed to have her as my life partner – as well as my teacher, role model, advisor, and my best friend. She is a true eshet chayil.

I would like to express my very great appreciation and hakarat hatov to my parents and mother-in-law. It is not possible to appropriately thank them in such a limited amount of space. After all, how is it possible to properly thank the people who have taken care of my wife and me since our first days in the world, and up until now? I am extremely fortunate to have such devoted and caring parents that can always be counted upon for guidance, support, and unconditional love.

I would also like to acknowledge and thank my children, for not only allowing me to take the time to create this book, but also for always making themselves available to lend their input and share their ideas and thoughts on ways of enhancing the book. I'm very proud of all my children and I pray that Hashem bless them with a life full of Torah, health, happiness, peace, and success.

I was also very fortunate to have an extra-special team of people who were responsible for actually producing this book. I am particularly grateful for the artistic design and creativity by the talented graphic artist, Stacey Gindi. I would like to express my appreciation for her beautiful work and creative thought, as well as her tireless effort and professionalism.

My special thanks are extended to the publisher, Moshe Kaufman, and the entire Israel Bookshop Publications staff. This project could not have been produced without their hard work, devotion, and expertise. I would like to offer my special thanks to the editor, Malkie Gendelman, for her patience, hard work, patience, skillful editing, and patience (can't say it enough!).

Of course, the greatest thanks of all goes to Hashem. I thank Hashem for allowing us to complete this project. I truly hope that this book will give people a glimpse of the Greatness of Hashem through the wonders of His creations.

Preface

Hashem said, "Let the waters teem with swarms of living creatures..." And Hashem created the great sea-giants and every living creature that creeps, with which the waters teem, of its kind... (*Bereishis* 1:20-21)

Whereas in our first book we explored various land animals, in this edition we will be traveling through the waters while exploring some of the most fascinating marine creatures in the animal kingdom.

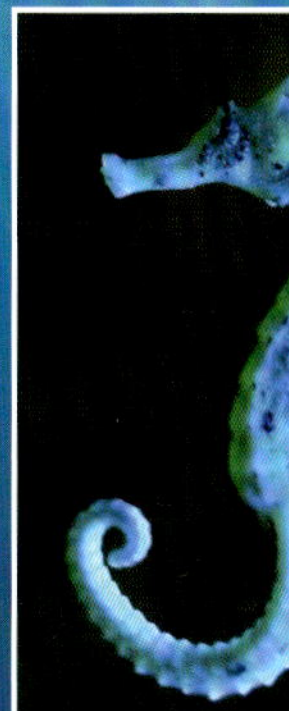

When most people think of marine animals or sea creatures, they usually think of fish. However, the underwater world is quite enormous and is populated with a large variety of diverse creatures. In fact, out of the thirty-five creatures that we will be visiting in this book, only eight are fish! The other creatures include amphibians, cephalopods, mammals, reptiles, and even aquatic birds.

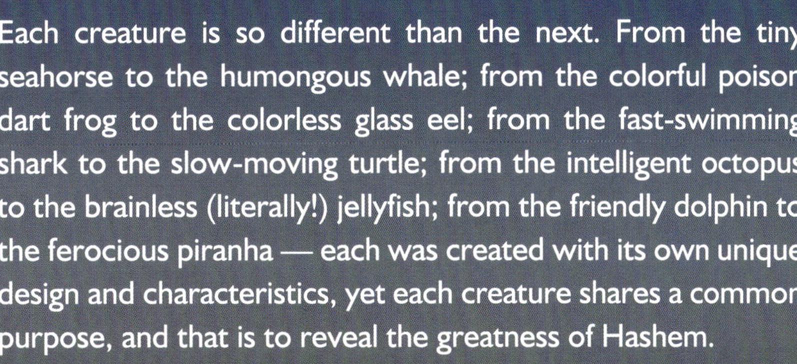

Just as the animal kingdom on the ground is full of great variety and design, the underwater world of animals is no less complex, just as fascinating — and much more mysterious.

Each creature is so different than the next. From the tiny seahorse to the humongous whale; from the colorful poison dart frog to the colorless glass eel; from the fast-swimming shark to the slow-moving turtle; from the intelligent octopus to the brainless (literally!) jellyfish; from the friendly dolphin to the ferocious piranha — each was created with its own unique design and characteristics, yet each creature shares a common purpose, and that is to reveal the greatness of Hashem.

Inside this book, we will take you on a spectacular underwater expedition, as we explore the oceans, seas, rivers, and lakes around the world, to learn the wonders and design of the aquatic members of the animal kingdom. Besides enjoying the incredible photos, you will learn fascinating facts and interesting insights about Hashem's amazing creatures.

Egg – Cellent!
Researchers have found a way to activate tumor-suppressor genes — and repress cancer growth — using an extract from the eggs of the axolotl.

AXOLOTL אקסולוטל

The Axolotl

The axolotl (pronounced ax-oh-lot-ul) is a very unique type of salamander that is found exclusively in the lake complex of Xochimilco (pronounced So-chee-mill-koh) near Mexico City. Unlike other salamanders, the axolotl retains its tadpole-like appearance for its entire life! Another difference between the axolotl and most other salamanders is the fact that the axolotl lives permanently in the water. Only in extremely rare cases will an axolotl metamorphose into a creature that can live on land, and emerge from the water (see "If Dry —Say Goodbye" section); most often, it is content to simply remain on the bottom of Xochimilco's lakes and canals.

The axolotl has a flat, broad head that is much wider than the rest of its body. It also has feathery gills which protrude from either side of its head, allowing it to breathe underwater. The axolotl is commonly found in albino form, completely lacking pigmentation. This makes the creature more visible to predators, which puts it at a much greater risk. For this reason, the axolotl spends a great deal of its life hiding under rocks and in crevices on the bottom of the lake. Axolotls are generally white or pink in color; however, black, gray, and brown ones can also be found. Axolotls can be quite large — they can reach up to fourteen inches in length — but their average size is closer to half of that.

The axolotl is a carnivorous animal, which means that it has a purely meat-based diet. This consists of worms and insect larvae that develop under the surface of the water, along with mollusks, crustaceans, and some small species of fish. The axolotl uses its sense of smell to locate its prey. Once it senses that food is nearby, it captures its prey by sucking it in with vacuum force.

Despite its relatively small size, the axolotl has surprisingly few natural predators, due to its bottom-of-the-water-dwelling lifestyle. The most common predators of the axolotl are large fish and birds, such as the heron, as well as humans who wish to catch these creatures to keep as pets in artificial environments.

The axolotl can live for up to twenty-five years, although on an average it rarely lives past the age of fifteen.

Today, the axolotl is considered to be a critically endangered species, meaning that there are very few axolotls left in the wild. Increasing levels of pollution, due to the ever-growing population of nearby Mexico City, is the most destructive factor to its survival.

Fast Fact:

The axolotl's name is taken from the Aztec language in which it means *water dog* ("atl" meaning *water*, and "xolotl" meaning *dog*).

Looks Fishy to Me

Australians and New Zealanders frequently refer to the axolotl as "the Mexican walking fish," because it looks like a fish that has hands and feet. However, the axolotl is actually not a fish at all, but rather a salamander, which is a type of amphibian.

Fish and amphibians are different in that a fish must live in the water to survive, while amphibians are born in the water but live on land and in water. Another major difference between the two is the fact that amphibians breathe using gills or spiracles when they are young and then develop lungs as they grow, while fish rely on gills for their breathing throughout their entire lives. Yet another difference is the fact that amphibians undergo metamorphosis as they grow from young to adult, changing from the egg stage to the larva phase and from that to adult form, while fish do not undergo this radical transformation.

Sticky Stuff

Female axolotls can lay 100 to 1,000 eggs every three to six months. Each egg is enveloped in mucus as it emerges. Coated with this sticky mucus, the eggs are able to stick to the plants and rocks in the water, which helps keep them safe. After about a month of the eggs' development, tiny axolotl babies emerge into the open water.

Gills and Thrills

Although the axolotl does develop rudimentary lungs, it still retains its branch-like gills, which is what it primarily uses to breathe from. The axolotl has three of these external gills projecting from either side of its neck. As water passes through these gills, the axolotl takes in oxygen from it. The gills are covered with feathery filaments, which increase the surface area for optimal gas exchange (taking in oxygen and giving off carbon dioxide).

Wacky Fact:

The axolotl has the unique ability to regenerate its spine and parts of its brain. It can also grow complete, new limbs after an original one becomes damaged or detached. If the axolotl loses its foot, for example, it will usually grow one back within a few weeks.

Forever Young

The axolotl exhibits an unusual trait known as neoteny. This is when an adult animal retains its juvenile features — in this case, the axolotl's larval-stage characteristics. The axolotl never metamorphoses. Because of this, even when it reaches adult form, it usually never fully resembles a regular adult salamander; it still retains its external gills, its tadpole-like dorsal fin that runs almost the length of its body, and its underdeveloped limbs.

Close Cousins

The closest relative of the axolotl is the tiger salamander. The tiger salamander is a small species of salamander that is found in wetland habitats across North America. The axolotl looks very similar to the larvae of the tiger salamander, and so people often confuse a young tiger salamander with the axolotl.

Adult tiger salamanders are rarely seen out in the open, as they spend their lives in burrows about two feet into the ground. Most adult tiger salamanders live in their burrows on the land, only returning to the water to find a mate. These salamanders are distinguishable from other species of salamanders by the dark-colored markings on their skin.

If Dry – Say Goodbye!

While the axolotl remains in a larval form throughout its life, it is able to metamorphose into a regular, adult Mexican salamander if its habitat dries up. It can actually change from a water-dwelling animal to a land-dwelling one! How does this occur?

Over a period of several weeks, the axolotl will slowly absorb its gills back into its body, while its lungs become strengthened and enlarged so that it can breathe oxygen from the atmosphere. The axolotl's tail changes from being flattened like a tadpole's to becoming more rounded like that of a true adult salamander, and its skin becomes tougher and dryer as the axolotl begins to adapt to living out of water. Eventually, its eyes begin to bulge out and develop eyelids.

Did You Know?

Because of their ability to regenerate lost body parts, axolotls are used extensively in scientific research.

When an amphibian such as a salamander or frog is in its tadpole stage, it is considered to be in its youth and cannot reproduce. However, the axolotl, while also an amphibian, is different. This remarkable creature has soft skin and four legs that resemble those of a lizard, but "fingers" and a large head that resemble those of a frog. By the dimensions of its body, it resembles a salamander, but its exterior appearance — black skin with dark brown spots on it — looks like that of the triton tadpole. Strangely enough, the axolotl can lay eggs while still in its original, tadpole-like state. And, while the axolotl can remain in this state for its entire life, it actually has the ability, in accordance with its surrounding conditions, to change into another creature — one that is called an ambystoma, which very much resembles a salamander.

A creature that changes into another creature in accordance with its surrounding conditions? Certainly something remarkable! But changing to adapt to its environment is necessary for the axolotl's survival, and so the Creator of the world implanted within it the amazing capacity to change.

For us, however, the opposite is true; in order to survive, a Jew must never change to adapt to his environment. Doing so would spell terrible catastrophe for us as a nation. The spiritual life of the Jew is permanent and not subject to change, regardless of the social, security, or economic conditions of the times.

Record Breaker:

While most axolotls live ten to fifteen years, there was an axolotl in Paris, France that lived for over twenty-five years, making it the oldest axolotl on record.

A common mistake is to assume that the axolotl is a lizard. A lizard, however, is a reptile, while the axolotl, like all salamanders, is an amphibian. One difference between the two is that reptiles, like humans, have four-chambered hearts while amphibians' hearts have only three chambers.

The jaw of the axolotl is equipped with fine teeth, which are used primarily for gripping prey, which the axolotl swallows whole.

The axolotl has poor eyesight, with no eyelids, and is very sensitive to light.

Today the axolotl is kept as a popular, freshwater aquarium pet all over the world.

The axolotl has short legs, with four digits on its front feet and five digits on its hind feet.

Like all amphibians, the axolotl is poikilothermic (its body temperature is dependent upon its surroundings).

Unlike some other neotenic salamanders, axolotls can be induced to metamorphose by an injection of iodine. The iodine stimulates the axolotl's thyroid and starts the metamorphosis process, which transforms the axolotl into an adult salamander. Unfortunately, axolotls that make this amazing transition often experience a shortened lifespan, most likely from the stress of the transformation.

Axolotl Trivia

1. Where do axolotls exist in the wild?
a. Canada **b.** Mexico **c.** China **d.** New York

2. The axolotl is…
a. a salamander **b.** an amphibian **c.** a carnivore **d.** a, b, and c

3. The axolotl is also known as…
a. the Mexican walking fish **b.** the Mexican walking amphibian
c. a tiger salamander **d.** a, b, and c

4. Which statement is false?
a. Axolotls come in various colors. **b.** Axolotls have external gills.
c. Axolotls have good eyesight. **d.** Axolotls can regenerate limbs.

5. The axolotl is closely related to which other animal?
a. Chinese giant salamander **b.** gecko **c.** tiger salamander **d.** toad

ANSWERS:
1. b 2. d 3. a 4. c 5. c

Animal Quackers:

Q. Why are axolotls always willing to give their friends a hand?
A. Because they can always grow another one!

Ouch!
Coral species may look like flowers, but they sting like a bee!

CORAL אלמוג

Coral

It may shock you to know that coral species are actually animals and a vital part of the marine world. These animal species are similar to the sea anemone (a group of water-dwelling, predatory animals that look like flowery plants) and almost appear to be half animal and half plant. Often mistaken for plants, coral are actually the limestone skeletons of tiny, spineless animals called coral polyps.

There are over 70,000 different species of coral that are found throughout the oceans of the world, though coral are particularly abundant in the southern hemisphere, due to the warm and tropical climates there.

Coral species are generally divided into two subspecies. They are categorized in accordance with how many tentacles each coral has. Coral species with eight tentacles are known as *Alcyonaria*, which includes soft coral, sea fans, and sea pens. Coral species with more than eight tentacles are known as *Zoantharia*, which includes the coral species that are found in coral reefs.

Coral obtain most of their nutrients from the algae that grow in the water. Algae depend on sunlight, which is why most coral, needing the sunlight indirectly, grow in clear and shallow water that is typically no deeper than 200 feet. There are, however, a number of coral species that have adapted to inhabiting the oceans at depths of up to 9,800 feet.

Coral are also known to catch small fish and animals such as plankton by using the stinging cells that they have on their tentacles.

Depending on the individual coral species and the role it plays within the ecosystem, coral can live from three months to thirty years. For example, there are coral species that make up extensive coral reefs and tend to live much longer than those species which are found on their own, like the softer corals.

Thousands of coral organisms live in a colony to form a coral reef. Coral reefs are bustling, underwater communities inhabited by thousands of species of animals and plants of various shapes, sizes, and colors. The coral polyps are the builders of the reefs.

Coral reefs play an enormous part in maintaining a high diversity of life in the world's oceans, as they not only provide excellent hideouts for marine animals seeking protection from oncoming predators, but also act as a meeting and breeding ground for literally thousands of species of animals, particularly fish.

Fast Fact:

Coral reefs occupy less than 0.1% of the world's ocean surface, yet they provide a home for 25% of all marine species.

Wet, Wild, &

Coral Reefs

Coral reefs are among the most colorful and interesting places in the sea. Often called "rainforests of the sea," coral reefs form some of the most diverse ecosystems on Earth.

Coral reefs along our coastlines are the richest habitats on the planet and are home to countless animal species. Creatures from many different groups, including invertebrates, echinoderms such as starfish and sea urchins, crustaceans, and reptiles, can be found inhabiting coral reef communities all around the world. Countless species of fish, including seahorses and eels, can also be spotted with ease there.

Other animals, such as the sea turtle, may not inhabit the coral reefs permanently, but will pay frequent visits there in order to find food. Sharks are the most commonly found predators around coral reefs, as they either feed there while they are passing or visit on a regular basis.

Coral reefs are made up of coral that exist with other animals, such as sponges and sea slugs. There are two main types of coral: hard coral and soft coral. Soft coral are individual animals (known as polyps) which move through the waters and eventually settle there. They may live in coral reefs, but these coral are not the ones that actually build the reefs. Hard coral are the reef-building coral. They often grow on top of the shells left behind by dead hard coral.

Coral reefs are found in the world's tropical and subtropical coastal regions, where it is always warm and never cool, even at night. The largest coral reefs can be found in the Caribbean, the southwest coast of Africa, all around southeast Asia and Australia, and throughout the coastal regions of the South Pacific Ocean. Because coral reefs are so rich in life and biodiversity, it is possible for so many different animal species to live together there without any competition for food.

Wacky Fact:

Many coral have been named for the objects they look like. For example: lettuce-leaf coral look like salad; boulder coral look like huge rocks; staghorn coral resemble the antlers of a deer; and the sea pen looks like a quill.

Wondrous

Coral Reef Fish

The coral reef fish are some of the most colorful and diverse creatures in the sea. Their wide range of bright colors and bold patterns is virtually unmatched in the entire undersea kingdom. Not only are these colors and designs beautiful to behold, but there is a real purpose behind each of them. Colors appear black underwater, which helps a fish swim around unseen. Stripes allow a fish to camouflage itself against the coral in the water. Spotted patterns serve to confuse a would-be predator. Each species of fish deals with survival in its own unique way. Below are a few examples of Hashem's magnificent creations that are found among the coral reef fish.

Pufferfish

The pufferfish normally has the appearance of a large tadpole, with bulging eyes and a long snout. There are around 120 known species of pufferfish, and most are poisonous. When the pufferfish is threatened, it inflates its body with air, exposing long, sharp, toxic spikes which normally intimidate the fish's predator. Although there are a number of other fish that prey on the pufferfish, these predators often meet with a nasty end. A predator will often be poisoned by the toxins in the pufferfish's spikes or the toxin that is released from the pufferfish's organs when it dies. Some creatures, however, such as sharks, are able to eat the pufferfish without being harmed.

Butterflyfish

The butterflyfish is well known for its brightly colored body and elaborate markings. Butterflyfish are diurnal creatures, which means that they are active and feed during the day and rest in the coral reef at night. Most species of butterflyfish (there are over 100 species of them) feed on plankton, sea anemones, coral, and small crustaceans. Due to the fact that butterflyfish are small in size, they are able to tuck themselves into crevices in the coral in order to escape danger and prevent themselves from being eaten by predators such as eels and sharks.

Lionfish

The lionfish is a poisonous, spiky, predatory fish. It hunts small fish, and its venom is capable of being fatal to larger creatures as well. The lionfish catches its prey by hiding in a crevice in the coral and then ambushing the prey as it swims by. The lionfish then corners the prey with its large fins, before swallowing it whole. The spikes that protrude from the lionfish's body contain venom, and if pursued, it will use its venomous spikes to defend itself.

Did You Know?

The pufferfish is the second most poisonous creature in the world (the most poisonous creature is the Golden Poison Frog).

The moments of dimness in the coral reefs are particularly active and exciting times. Each reef contains a wide variety of creatures, all of which have different living patterns and lifestyles. It is no wonder, then, that the transition from daytime to nighttime and vice versa, until these creatures become accustomed to the dark of the night or the light of the new day, turns the place into a most intriguing scene. Over the course of this period, the reef becomes like a traffic jam in a major city with no police officers, traffic lights, or protocol. Dozens of groups of creatures change their modes of activity drastically during these moments.

Most of the creatures begin swimming frantically and stop eating. Their colors begin to fade. Other creatures, those of prey, take advantage of the traffic and confusion to catch some food. Then night settles in, the sea life becomes accustomed to the darkness, and normalcy returns.

With daybreak, the process begins once again; chaos and confusion reign as the darkness of night gives way to the new day. Fifteen minutes after sunrise, though, the day has officially begun and life in the coral reef gradually returns to normal.

These moments of dimness are a time of total blur and confusion, and it exists in our world, as well. We, too, experience periods of unsettledness, periods during which we feel the weight of the brazenness and cruelty that permeate the world. We are left dumbfounded by the falsehood that pervades daily life, by the darkness and confusion brought on by our current exile.

This is a time when a person is confronted with a few choices: to remain passive and be caught by the various forces and missionaries around him, or to run away and close his eyes to all the chaos surrounding his life. Yet another option, though, is for the person to take the initiative and decide to attach himself unconditionally to the one, singular Truth, that of the Torah and mitzvos.

As Jews, we know that the confusion we experience in this world signals the coming of Mashiach, and that when he finally comes, the sun will shine with utmost brilliance and scatter all the clouds of confusion for good. Then the light of Mashiach will glow, and the preoccupation of the entire world will be with nothing but the knowledge of Hashem.

Record Breaker:

The largest coral reef in the world, the Great Barrier Reef, stretches more than 1,200 miles, from New Guinea southward along the east coast of Australia. It comprises over 2,900 individual reefs and 900 islands!

INTERESTING FACTS & STATS

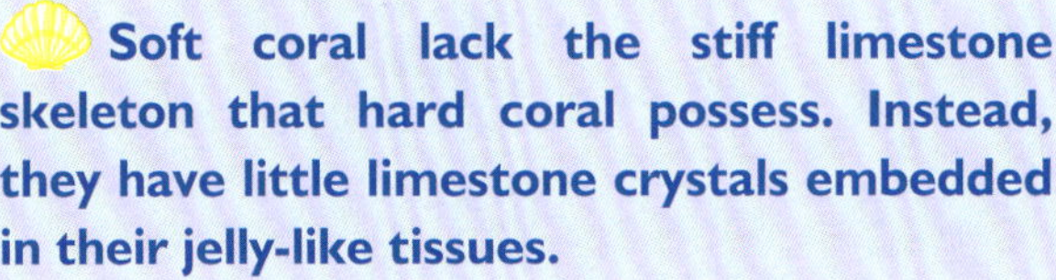

Soft coral lack the stiff limestone skeleton that hard coral possess. Instead, they have little limestone crystals embedded in their jelly-like tissues.

Hard coral will attach themselves to a spot on the sea floor and then remain growing there, in that same spot, for the rest of their life.

Some types of coral are made into jewelry; the coral most often used for this purpose is the precious coral, or red coral, found in the Mediterranean Sea and the Sea of Japan.

Coral reefs protect coastlines from waves that may cause erosion.

Coral reefs are second only to rainforests in biodiversity of species.

Various types of microscopic algae, known as *Symbiodinium*, live inside of coral, providing the coral with food and helping them to grow faster.

It has been predicted by researchers that over 50% of the world's coral formations will have disappeared by the year 2030, and surprisingly, not just due to pollution and commercial fishing. Storms and natural disasters such as earthquakes and tsunamis have a devastating effect on coral reefs, as well.

Coral Trivia

1. What is a coral?
a. a type of animal **b.** a type of plant **c.** a type of bacteria **d.** a, b, and c

2. Coral have…
a. fins **b.** gills **c.** tentacles **d.** feet

3. Which statement is false?
a. Coral reefs are found mostly in shallow water. **b.** Coral turn white when stressed.
c. Coral can live up to thirty years. **d.** Coral reefs grow best in the Arctic.

4. What is the coral's favorite food?
a. crustaceans **b.** plankton **c.** starfish **d.** shark bait

5. How do coral reefs directly help the environment?
a. They protect small fish from predators. **b.** Their beautiful colors enhance the ocean floor.
c. They protect the coastal areas from storms and powerful waves.

ANSWERS: 1. a 2. c 3. d 4. b 5. c

Animal Quackers:

Q. What would happen if you threw a yellow-colored coral into the Red Sea?
A. It would get wet.

Say Ahhh!
A crocodile cannot stick out its tongue, as its tongue is attached to the top of its mouth.

CROCODILE תנין

The Crocodile

Crocodiles, alligators, caimans, and gharials (or gavials) are reptiles that belong to the group known as crocodilians. Crocodilians are water-dwelling animals that prefer to live in large bodies of shallow water, sluggish rivers, and open swamps. They have large, lizard-shaped bodies; long snouts; tough, scaled hides; sharp teeth; and two pairs of short legs. Their feet are webbed, so they can walk easily on the soft, wet ground. They have long, strong tails which enable them to swim and move about in the water. On land they can run for short, rapid bursts, but they get tired very quickly. They can also execute several-meter-long jumps out of the water. The saltwater and Nile crocodiles of Africa are the largest, as well as the most vicious, of the crocodilians.

Crocodiles live throughout the watery tropics of Africa, Asia, America, and Australia. They can swim as fast as twenty-five miles per hour and are able to stay underwater for two to three hours at a time. As wacky as it sounds, crocodiles are known to swallow stones when they are on the banks of the water. Doing so helps their digestive systems and also contributes to their water buoyancy. Additionally, it is thought that by swallowing stones, crocodiles may also be able to swim to deeper parts of the water.

Crocodiles are ambush hunters; they wait for fish or land animals to come close and then rush out to attack them. As cold-blooded predators, they have very slow metabolisms, so they can survive long periods without food. Despite their appearance of being slow, crocodiles are top predators in their environment. They feed on fish, other reptiles, birds, and mammals. Occasionally, large crocodiles may attack large animals and people, too.

The female crocodile lays twenty to eighty eggs at a time. Incredibly, when it is time for the eggs to hatch, the baby crocodiles inside grow an "egg tooth," a point at the end of their noses that they use to break through their shells so that they can get out. After a baby crocodile has hatched from its egg, its "egg tooth" slowly disappears.

Most of the crocodile offspring are eaten in the first year of their lives by large fish, monitor lizards, hyenas, storks, herons, adult crocodiles, and even humans. The surviving crocodiles can live up to eighty years in the wild.

Fast Fact:

The saltwater crocodile can outrun a galloping horse!

Wet, Wild, &

Lessons Learned

It is said that crocodiles keep on growing, albeit more slowly as they get older, until they die. That's why crocodiles are such big animals.

Learning and spiritual growth are also lifelong processes, those that we should constantly be striving to improve ourselves in. While it is wonderful to be satisfied with our physical possessions, we should never be content with the level of spirituality that we are on. Instead, we should endeavor to continually improve ourselves and keep on growing. This way we can become outstanding people and truly reach the potential given to us by our Creator.

Building a Nest Egg

Baby croc hatching from egg

Like other reptiles, all crocodiles lay eggs in nests built on the land. Some crocs build a mound from vegetation and mud, and then dig a hole in the top, into which they lay their eggs before covering them over. Other species simply dig a hole in the sand and lay their eggs in the cavity. While most reptiles lay their eggs and then move on, mother and father crocs ferociously guard their nests until the eggs hatch.

When the eggs are ready to be hatched, the baby crocodiles emit high-pitched cries. The mother crocodile hears the cries and digs the eggs out. Some croc moms even help the hatchlings escape out of their shells by gently biting the eggs! Once the babies hatch, the mother crocodile places the hatchlings in her mouth and carries them to the water. She then remains with her young for several months.

SUPER Crocs

Scientists in the United States have isolated a powerful agent in crocodile blood which could help conquer human infections that are immune to standard antibiotics. The discovery was made thanks to the curiosity of a producer filming a documentary on saltwater crocodiles in Australia. Realizing that crocs heal very quickly and rarely get infections, the producer wondered how their immune system works.

A leading research institute drew crocodile blood and tested it on a number of strains of bacteria, including newer, drug-resistant bacteria. When a drop of crocodile blood was placed right in the middle of a culture dish of bacteria, it killed all the bacteria near it.

Wacky Fact:

A mother crocodile can carry her young in a pouch inside her mouth.

The Saltwater Crocodile

The saltwater crocodile is the largest of all crocodilians. Average-size males reach seventeen feet and weigh 1,000 pounds, but specimens over twenty feet long and weighing 2,200 pounds are not uncommon. Saltwater crocs are excellent swimmers and have often been spotted far out at sea. They'll feed on anything they can get their jaws on, including water buffalo, monkeys, wild boar, and even sharks! Without warning, these crocodiles will explode from the water with a thrash of their powerful tails, grasp their victim, and drag it back in, holding it underwater until the animal drowns. Saltwater crocs also have a long history of attacking and consuming humans who stray into their territory.

Dwarf Crocodile

The dwarf crocodile is the smallest species of crocodile in the world, rarely longer than 5.5 feet. It is natively found in the rainforests of West Africa. The dwarf crocodile's very distinct features include a short, broad snout and tough scales that cover its entire black body (most crocodiles do not have such armored scales on their undersides). These characteristics have led to the dwarf crocodile being known by a number of different names, including the broad-snouted crocodile, the bony crocodile, and the black crocodile.

Crocs vs. Gators

While crocodiles are often confused with alligators, they belong to two separate taxonomic families. Although they are both reptiles and are both crocodilians, there are a number of differences which set these predators apart.

- Crocodiles have a longer, more V-shaped head than alligators.
- The fourth tooth of a crocodile sticks out when its mouth is closed, which is not the case with alligators.
- Crocodiles are better adapted to living in seawater than are alligators.
- Crocodiles are more aggressive than alligators.
- Crocodiles tend to have a lighter appearance than alligators.
- Crocodiles in the wild are found all over the world, while alligators are only found in the U.S. and China.

American Alligator

Did You Know?

Crocodiles have the strongest bite of any animal in the world.

The crocodile was considered sacred by the ancient Egyptians, and Pharaoh himself was worshipped by the Egyptians as the "great crocodile" (*Yechezkel* 29:3). The Nile crocodile reigns supreme in its river, and Pharaoh reigned supreme in his vast empire, becoming quite arrogant and vicious and refusing to acknowledge a Higher Authority, until he experienced the Ten Plagues.

The second plague which battered the Egyptians was the proliferation of the *tzefardei'a* throughout the land. While the word *tzefardei'a* is popularly understood to mean "frog," there are some *mefarshim*, such as the Abarbanel and Rabbeinu Chananel, who hold that the proper translation of the word *tzefardei'a* is "crocodile" — ouch!

Some reasons why *tzefardei'a* is translated as "crocodile" are:

1. The Egyptians worshipped a crocodile god. Therefore, in keeping with the purpose of the plagues, which was not only to punish but also to educate, the Egyptians were attacked by their very own god. This demonstrated Hashem's mastery over the Egyptian god.

2. The verse in *Tehillim* (78:45) says that Hashem sent *wild animals which consumed them, and* tzefardei'a *which destroyed them.* Frogs are not generally creatures of destruction, whereas crocodiles are.

Most commentaries, however, disagree with this interpretation of the word *tzefardei'a*, for several reasons:

In describing the *tzefardei'a*, the Torah writes (*Shemos* 7:28), *They will come into your houses, your bedrooms, and your beds...* The verse implies that the presence of the *tzefardei'a* were the only source of the Egyptians' suffering. If it were a crocodile plague, the Egyptians' suffering would consist of much more than the fact that the *tzefardei'a* filled their houses.

The *tzefardei'a* are described as "swarming," which usually implies small creatures.

Our Sages say that one aspect of the plague of *tzefardei'a* was the incessant, maddening croaking noise that the creatures made. Frogs croak, whereas crocodiles just smile.

It is interesting to note yet another opinion, brought down in the *Ha'amek Davar* (*Shemos* 7:29), which suggests that *tzefardei'a* refers to both frogs and crocodiles, with frogs infesting all of Egypt and crocodiles infesting just Pharaoh's palace.

Record Breaker:

The largest crocodile in captivity was Lolong, a saltwater crocodile that measured 20.24 feet and weighed 2,370 pounds, and was caught in the Philippines. Before its capture, Lolong was suspected of killing and consuming two people.

The term "crying crocodile tears" — which refers to displaying fake sadness — comes from the myth that crocodiles weep when eating their victims, or that they cry in order to lure their prey. They do wipe their eyes when eating, but only because eating causes their eyes to bubble and froth.

When crocodiles sit on river banks with their mouths open, it's not aggression. They are cooling off by releasing heat through their mouths, since they do not have sweat glands.

Crocodiles can eat their prey underwater; their throats have the ability to keep from swallowing water while they eat there.

A crocodile has twenty-four teeth. When it loses a tooth, the tooth grows back very quickly.

Crocodiles have the ability to keep their eyes open underwater.

Crocodiles close their nostrils while underwater.

A healthy crocodile can live up to two years without eating anything! It is able to lower its metabolism rate to such an extreme point that it does not need much energy to stay alive.

The crocodile is one of the few living creatures that naturally preys on humans.

Crocodile Trivia

1. Why do crocodiles keep their mouths open while resting in the river banks?
a. to scare predators **b.** to greet their mates **c.** to catch prey **d.** to cool off

2. Which of the following statements is false?
a. Crocodiles do not have sweat glands. **b.** A crocodile can eat a shark.
c. Crocodiles are fast swimmers. **d.** Crocodiles are only found in the United States.

3. Which is the largest crocodile?
a. Nile crocodile **b.** saltwater crocodile **c.** black crocodile **d.** American crocodile

4. How is the crocodile able to digest all the bones and shells that it consumes?
a. It has very sharp teeth. **b.** It consumes a lot of water while it eats.
c. Its stomach is very acidic. **d.** It doesn't sleep for days at a time after it finishes a meal.

5. The crocodile got its name from the Greeks. What does it mean?
a. worm of stones **b.** great lizard **c.** wild beast **d.** large reptile

Animal Quackers:

Q. What do you call a crocodile that just finished eating a frog?
A. A croak-odile.

DOLPHIN דולפין

The Dolphin

Even though they live in the ocean all of the time, dolphins are mammals, not fish. Like every mammal, dolphins are warm-blooded. Unlike fish, which breathe through gills, dolphins breathe air using their lungs. Other characteristics of dolphins that separate them from fish are that they give birth to live young rather than laying eggs, and that they feed their young milk.

The dolphin is considered to be one of the most intelligent creatures on earth. Dolphins are also very entertaining and friendly. They enjoy playing and socializing with other dolphins from their pod (group of dolphins), as well as with people. For fun, they will play with items found in the water, such as seaweed. Sometimes, they will even tease other living creatures in the water just for the amusement of it.

Dolphins belong to a group of mammals called cetaceans. Whales are also included in this group; as a matter of fact, dolphins are referred to as "toothed whales." There are about forty species of dolphins, and they can be found swimming in our oceans worldwide.

The dolphin's senses are very highly developed. Their hearing, eyesight, and sense of touch are excellent. They rely on their acute senses to avoid threats, to socialize, and to hunt for food. The sense of touch is essential for dolphins, as they use it for bonding within their pods. Dolphins have been observed caring for their sick, elderly, and injured. The dolphin's sense of smell, however, is limited.

The body of a dolphin is designed to help it travel through the waters quickly and effortlessly. Its pectoral fins (flippers) and its fluke (tail) help it to navigate through the ocean, where it can swim for long periods of time at a speed of up to twenty-five miles per hour. Dolphins' colors vary, but these sea mammals are generally gray, with their backs darker than the rest of their bodies.

Because the various species of dolphins are so diverse, they range in size. Maui's dolphin, the smallest of all dolphins, is around four feet long, and weighs around ninety pounds. The boto, the largest dolphin that lives in freshwater, can be up to ten feet long, and weighs up to 400 pounds. The largest species of dolphin, the orca, or killer whale, can grow to about twenty-five feet in length, and weighs about 19,000 pounds!

Fast Fact:

The dolphin is the only mammal that gives birth to its young tail-first instead of head-first.

Wet, Wild, &

A Calf Is Born...

Female dolphins give birth every two to three years. After a twelve-month pregnancy, the mother dolphin will usually give birth to one calf; twins are rare. As soon as the calf is born, the mother quickly takes it up to the surface, so that it can take its first breath. The calf will nurse for up to eighteen months, and it will remain with its mother for three to eight years. During this period, the young dolphin will learn the necessary skills that it will need to survive when it becomes a mature adult.

The Bottlenose Dolphin

The bottlenose dolphin is the most common and well-known type of dolphin, and can be found in warm seas worldwide. They are called bottlenose dolphins because their beaks are shaped like bottles. Bottlenose dolphins are gray in color and are eight to thirteen feet long. They swim in large groups that include fifteen to over a thousand dolphins per pod.

Bottlenose dolphins are extremely intelligent and are able to send messages to one another in different ways. Their forms of communication include squeaking, whistling, snapping their jaws, and slapping their tails on the surface of the water. These dolphins are acrobatic as well, and can jump over twenty feet in the air!

Teamwork

Dolphins often team up with other members of their pod to hunt for food. They work very well as a team and use various methods to catch their prey. Dolphins' hunting tactics include circling a school of fish, which causes the fish to swim close together, forming a tight ball. Then the dolphins take turns swimming through the center of the ball of fish to snap the fish up and eat them! Dolphins will also follow seabirds, whales, and fishing boats in order to feed on the fish they scare away or discard.

Wacky Fact:

Only half of the dolphin's brain sleeps at a time! The other half remains awake, allowing the dolphin to breathe (preventing it from drowning) and to stay alert in case of danger.

Wondrous

Seeing under the Sea

Although dolphins have very good vision, they locate their food through *echolocation*, which refers to an ability dolphins have that allows them to "see" with their ears by listening for echoes. Dolphins produce a high-frequency clicking sound, which acts as a sonar system. When the clicking sounds hit an object in the water, like a fish or rock, the sound waves bounce off the object and return to the dolphin in the form of an echo. The returning sound is received in the fatty portions of the dolphin's lower jaw and is then sent to the ear and to the brain for analysis. Through this echolocation, dolphins are able to determine the size, shape, direction, and speed of objects in the water.

Armed and Dangerous

In the early 1960s, the U.S. Navy began training marine mammals for military purposes. Bottlenose dolphins were used in combat for various tasks including:

Locating sea mines: The dolphins would locate a mine and deposit a weighted buoy line near it in order to mark its location. In the 2003 Gulf War, dolphins helped neutralize more than 100 mines in the Iraqi harbors.

Detecting and marking enemy divers: This procedure was used in the Vietnam War and the Persian Gulf War to protect Navy anchored vessels from enemy swimmers seeking to plant explosives. Dolphins would patrol the area and alert their trainer if they located a swimmer.

Nowadays, dolphins are also trained to "tag" enemy swimmers with a marker, so that Navy personnel can later apprehend these swimmers.

Killing our enemies: During the Vietnam War, rumors circulated that dolphins were being trained to shoot at enemy swimmers with a device similar to the tagging device. However, the Navy denies that any such program existed.

Did You Know?

The brain of a bottlenose dolphin is larger than a human brain!

There was once a fisherman who owned a large marina. One day, he trapped a dolphin who wandered inside his marina. The dolphin promised the fisherman three wise teachings in exchange for his release. Knowing that dolphins are said to be intelligent creatures, the fisherman agreed to the dolphin's proposal and let it go free.

Safely out of the fisherman's reach, the dolphin said, "If you live your life by the following three teachings, you will become wealthy, powerful, and wise. 1) Always be satisfied with your lot. 2) Never become angry. 3) Observe life so you will be able to learn from others." Then the dolphin burst into laughter and said to the fisherman, "You should know, had you not let me go, you would have found inside of me a pearl the size of a watermelon!"

Enraged, the fisherman yelled, "You're just a silly dolphin! What do you know?!" He jumped into the water and swam after the dolphin. The dolphin dove deep into the sea, but the fisherman followed frantically. The dolphin continued to descend deeper and deeper into the sea until the fisherman was no longer able to hold his breath. Forced to come up for air, the fisherman pulled himself out of the sea and collapsed to the ground. Catching his breath, he slowly got up and stared angrily at the dolphin.

The dolphin answered his stare with the following rebuke: "You fool, I was only testing you to see if you would heed my advice. You have failed miserably. I told you to always be satisfied with your lot, yet you risked your life for a phantom pearl. The truly wealthy person is someone who finds satisfaction in what he already has.

"I told you to never lose your temper, but as soon as you thought you were duped, you became so enraged that you actually thought you had a chance to catch me with your bare hands. The most powerful person is the one who can control himself and overcome his urges. Power is not a measure of physical strength; rather it is the ability to maintain self-control at all times.

"I told you to observe life so you would be able to learn from others, but as soon as I finished giving you pearls of wisdom, you ignored what I had to say because you thought you knew better. A wise person does not put anyone down and does not judge others by their status or class in society."

Record Breaker:

A "stampede" of about 2,000 short-beaked common dolphins was spotted swimming in southern California in February 2011.

- The dorsal fin (fin located on the back) of each dolphin is very unique, and it can be used to identify one dolphin from another.
- There are about 100 teeth in the mouth of a dolphin, which they use to grab their prey. But they don't chew the prey; all of their food is swallowed whole.
- The dolphin's name originates from the ancient Greek word *delphís*, meaning "womb." The animal's name can therefore be defined as "a fish with a womb."
- Bottlenose dolphins look like they might be grinning. Their smiles are formed by the way their mouths curve.
- Dolphins must make frequent trips to the surface of the water to catch their breath. The blowhole on top of a dolphin's head acts as a "nose."
- Dolphins need to get air at various intervals. Some need air every twenty seconds, while others only need it every thirty minutes.
- Researchers believe that dolphins conserve energy by swimming alongside ships, a practice known as bow-riding.
- A dolphin may be able to dive up to 1,000 feet.
- Dolphins mostly eat fish and squid.

Dolphin Trivia

1. Dolphins travel in groups called…
a. schools **b.** herds **c.** pods **d.** gangs

2. Excluding humans, which creature has the highest EQ (the ratio of brain size to body size) on the planet?
a. a killer whale **b.** a chimpanzee **c.** a gorilla **d.** a bottlenose dolphin

3. Which one of these creatures is not a dolphin?
a. boto **b.** killer whale **c.** narwhal **d.** They are all dolphins.

4. Which statement is false?
a. Dolphins have excellent vision. **b.** Dolphins have a good sense of hearing.
c. Dolphins have a good sense of smell. **d.** Dolphins are mammals.

5. What is the tail of the dolphin called?
a. fin **b.** fluke **c.** flipper **d.** flounder

ANSWERS:
1. c 2. d 3. d 4. c 5. b

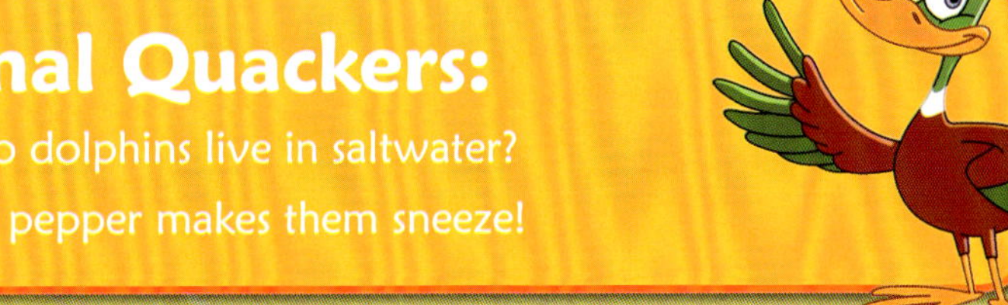

Animal Quackers:

Q. Why do dolphins live in saltwater?

A. Because pepper makes them sneeze!

Quack...Quack...
Contrary to a popular myth, the duck's quack does indeed echo.

DUCK ברווז

The Duck

Ducks are medium-sized aquatic birds that are related to swans and geese. Ducks, however, are smaller in size, and differ from swans and geese in their tendency to dive into the water in order to catch food. Overall, there are 150 different species of duck; all are part of the bird family *Anatidae*.

Ducks come in a variety of contrasting colors, from bright and beautiful to dull and drab. Colors include bright greens, striking bronzes, and beautiful purples, as well as boring grays, dull whites, and dreary browns. The male duck is usually more brightly colored than the female.

The duck swims very gracefully in water, but on land it walks with a comical and clumsy waddle. It is an excellent flier; some ducks can fly as fast as sixty miles per hour. The duck has thick, soft feathers which are made water-repellent by a film of oil that the duck, using its bill, presses out of a gland located just above its tail. Water cannot penetrate this film, and it prevents the duck from becoming wet and cold. A duck's feathers are so waterproof that even when the duck dives underwater, its downy under-layer of feathers will stay completely dry.

Ducks are omnivorous birds, and each species has its own dietary requirements. They are able to feed in and out of water. Some will dive underwater to catch fish, others feed in corn fields and marshes, and others eat along the banks of lakes and rivers. In general, ducks will feed on aquatic plants, seeds, nuts, berries, insects, worms, leeches, frogs, shell fish, salamanders, and small fish.

Ducks are found in both seawater and freshwater. Their ability to adapt to different conditions and to eat such diverse foods is what makes the duck one of the most widespread birds in the world; they are found on every continent, with the exception of Antarctica.

The duck, however, is very vulnerable to its many predators. Predators include foxes, wolves, large fish, and crocodiles. Ducks are also hunted regularly by humans. Because of its calm and quiet nature, it often takes a long time for the duck to react to surrounding noise, which makes it an easy target for those wishing to attack it.

Ducks are farmed all over the world for their meat and eggs. They are also farmed for their feathers (known as down), which are most commonly used in bedding such as quilts and pillows.

Fast Fact:

Mallard ducks are known to have the longest migration period of any duck, extending from late summer to early winter.

Egg-Cetra...

Female ducks of most species lay six to twelve eggs at a time (though some species lay as many as twenty eggs at a time). Duck eggshells have 7,500 pores on their surfaces. Respiratory gasses, as well as water vapor, travel through these pores, allowing the baby egg inside to breathe.

Generally, only the mother duck incubates the eggs. When the mother leaves the nest, she covers the eggs with a layer of feathers. Incubation lasts for about a month. After hatching, the young ducks follow their mother to a body of water. Most ducklings first fly between fifty and sixty days old.

Bills, Bills, Bills...

Ducks do not have teeth, so they use their spoon-shaped bills to catch their food. A duck's bill is specialized to help it forage in mud and strain food from the water. A hard nail at the tip of the bill helps with the foraging, and a comb-like structure on the sides of the bill helps with the straining of nutrients, insects, and shellfish from the water. This comb-like structure, called a *pecten*, is also used by the duck to pick the dirt out of its feathers.

The species of ducks that feed on fish have long, rough, and strongly serrated bills, which are needed to catch prey and to prevent it from escaping.

Webbed Waddlers

Ducks have webbed feet which act as paddles, allowing them to swim fast and smoothly in the water. When ducks swim, they push their feet out in a kicking motion so that the webbing catches the water and pushes it behind the duck. On the return stroke, the webbing on the foot of the duck closes up, which allows the duck to have less water resistance and thus be able to travel faster. The duck's webbed feet are well designed for swimming and for walking on slippery river banks, but not so much for walking on dry land. That is why ducks waddle when they walk.

Wacky Fact:

Ducks do not have blood vessels or nerves in their feet! This is why their feet cannot feel the cold, even when they're swimming in icy waters.

The Mallard Duck

The mallard is the most common and familiar duck in the world. The mallard's yellow bill, white neck ring, rich chestnut breast, and green head distinguish it from all other ducks. The female has mottled brown plumage, with a whitish tail. Mallards prefer calm, shallow waters, but can be found in almost any body of water across Asia, Europe, and North America. The females quack loudly and often, while the males just make a single, faint sound. Mallards grow to about twenty-six inches in length, weigh up to three pounds, and can live up to ten years in the wild.

The Wood Duck

The wood duck is one of the most beautiful ducks in the world. It has purple wings and a metallic-green head marked with white lines. Unlike most ducks, wood ducks nest in hollow trees. They live in wooded swamps, marshes, and small lakes. They are one of the few duck species with claws; thus they can grip bark and sit atop branches. They build their nests directly over the water, though at times their nests can be up to one mile away from the water. After hatching, the ducklings jump down from the nest tree and make their way to the pond or lake. These ducklings are able to jump from heights of up to 300 feet!

The Hooded Merganser

The hooded merganser is a small duck that has a collapsible crest made of feathers. When the feathers lie flat, they look like hair. But when the feathers are raised, they look like a hood, making the duck's head look oversized and oblong.

The hooded merganser is an excellent diver. It is able to see clearly underwater and search for its prey. Amazingly, it has the ability to change the refractive properties of its eyes in order to enhance its underwater vision. It also has an extra eyelid, called a "nictitating membrane," which acts as a pair of transparent goggles, as it provides added protection to the eye.

Did You Know?

Contrary to popular belief, not all ducks quack! Most male ducks are silent, and it is only the females of most duck species that actually make a quacking sound. Other duck sounds include whistles, squeaks, grunts, chirps, and growls.

Watching a male duck swimming in the lake, with its bright and colorful feathers and its graceful demeanor in the water, is truly a beautiful sight to behold. But the duck's talents are not relegated to its looks — the duck has many more attributes to offer. In the air, it is an agile flier; and in the water, it is an elegant swimmer. It is also blessed with amazingly waterproof feathers. Yes, the duck certainly has a lot to quack about — but that is exactly the one thing that it does not do! The male duck does not quack; only the female duck does.

What an important lesson for us to learn. So often, when a person is blessed with exceptional wisdom, strength, beauty, or other Heavenly-bestowed gifts, he instinctively feels the need to boast about it and let others know how great he is for having such talents and abilities. However, we must realize that we have nothing to do with the gifts that Hashem has bestowed upon us; we did nothing to acquire them, and as such, how can we brag about them? Boasting about our talents is really no different from gloating over our ability to breathe or to eat or walk, as these are all blessings from Hashem that don't have anything to do with our own personal achievements.

Instead of bragging about our talents, we should be silent as the beautiful male duck that does not quack, and instead focus on thanking Hashem for the gifts He gave us. Additionally, we should realize that the more Heavenly gifts we have been blessed with, the more responsibility we have to utilize those gifts in ways that bring glory to our Creator, the One from Whom we receive all life and blessing.

If we do this, we will have achieved the sterling quality that the Torah holds in such high regard — true humility.

Record Breaker:

In April 2010, a mallard duck had twenty-one hatchlings, setting a new world record for the most ducklings hatched at once.

An adult male duck is called a drake, and the female duck is called a hen. There are many different names given to a group of ducks, such as: raft, team, brace, flock, paddling, and badling.

Baby ducks are precocial, meaning they are born relatively mature and are independently mobile after hatching. Ducklings are born with their eyes wide open and with a warm layer of down. They are able to leave the nest within hours of hatching.

Ducklings can swim right away, but it takes about two months before they can fly.

Ducks have very good vision, and they can see in color.

A typical duck's nest is built on the ground, usually in some depression among reeds or stones or in a cavity of a dead tree. Some ducks, however, build their nests high up inside a hollow section of a tree.

Ducklings emerge from their eggs by using a specialized, hardened "egg tooth" to help them break through their shell.

Ducks are particularly clean animals that keep their nests free of waste and debris. They enjoy preening their feathers and showing off their beautiful plumage.

Toward the end of the summer, male ducks begin to lose their feathers. New feathers grow back within about a month.

Duck Trivia

1. There are 150 species of duck. Which duck is the most common?
a. wood duck **b.** Daffy duck **c.** Mandarin duck **d.** mallard duck

2. Which factor allows the duck to fly long distances?
a. its powerful wings **b.** its webbed feet **c.** its diet **d.** its ability to swim

3. Some ducks have groove-like notches on the edges of their bills. How do ducks use these serrated bills?
a. to fight off predators **b.** to hold their prey **c.** to dive underwater **d.** to whistle loudly

4. What is the average size of the mallard duck?
a. five to nine inches **b.** ten to twelve inches **c.** thirteen to eighteen inches **d.** twenty to twenty-six inches

5. Which statement concerning the duck is false?
a. It is related to the goose. **b.** It can see colors.
c. Ducks can be found in all seven continents in the world. **d.** All ducks do not quack.

ANSWERS: 1.d 2.a 3.b 4.d 5.c

Animal Quackers:

Q. What do you get when you put six ducks in a box?

A. A box of quackers!

Believe It or Not:
Eels can actually crawl across land to get to other ponds and rivers.
EEL
צלופח

The Eel

Eels are known for their long, snake-like bodies. Although they sure look like snakes, eels are actually fish and come from the order *Anguilliformes*. Their spinal column consists of more than 100 vertebrae, which gives them great flexibility. There are close to 800 species of eels in the world, ranging in length from two inches to thirteen feet. All eels have elongated, narrow bodies with long dorsal and anal fins that often extend over most of their body length. (The dorsal fin is located on its back, while the anal fin is located at its bottom.)

Most species of eels live in the shallow waters of the ocean and burrow into sand or mud or among rocky crevices. Sometimes, eels can be found living together in holes, or "eel pits." Eels are usually ambush predators, hiding in their burrows or coral reefs in wait of their prey. Some eels, however, are more aggressive hunters and pursue their prey by using their long bodies to reach into holes and crevices.

The moray eel is perhaps the most well-known eel, with close to 200 species of it occupying both deep and shallow tropical oceans worldwide. Moray eels tend to remain in the crevices deep in the ocean rather than venturing onto shore. The largest populations of moray eels are found around tropical coral reefs.

Moray eels generally reach five feet in length, but can grow to lengths of ten feet. They vary from each other in both size and color, but all moray eels are fairly similar in appearance. They have large eyes; a mouth that contains large, sharp, backward-curving teeth that can inflict serious wounds; and an elongated body that is slightly flattened toward the tail.

The moray eel is a carnivorous creature and is often one of the most dominant predators within its environment. It is a nocturnal hunter which preys on other eels, fish, crustaceans such as crabs, and mollusks including squid and cuttlefish. Even though the moray eel has poor hearing and eyesight, it has an acute sense of smell, which makes it such a formidable predator. The moray eel, however, has its own predators to be wary of — such as groupers, barracudas, sharks, and larger moray eels. But since it spends the majority of its time hiding, it is able to remain out of sight from predators and at the same time be in a position to ambush any unsuspecting prey that passes by it.

Fast Fact:

Humans do not generally hunt moray eels, as many of the species are toxic to us.

Fins and Skins

Although it seemingly has both signs that indicate that it is a kosher fish — fins and scales — the eel is not kosher. This is because not all scales are considered to be a "kosher sign." In order to be considered a "kosher sign," the scale must be easily removable without damaging the fish's skin. Bony tubercles and plate-like or thorn-like scales that can be removed only by removing part of the skin with them are not considered scales in this context. Since the eel's "scales" fall into this category — they are part of the eel's skin and cannot be easily removed — the eel is not kosher.

Most Mysterious Migration

Every year European eels make one of nature's most amazing migrations. European eels are catadromous fish, which means that they live in freshwater but enter saltwater to spawn (lay their eggs).

These eels' eggs hatch in the Sargasso Sea, a warm-water area of the North Atlantic Ocean, and the baby eels begin their life as larvae called *leptocephali*. At that point, they are small, flat, transparent, and shaped like a willow leaf. They remain in this state for twelve months, while they float thousands of miles to coasts from Iceland to Europe and North Africa. After the larval phase, they metamorphose into transparent "glass eels," taking on the shape of an eel and growing to be about two or three inches long. They swim into estuaries (partially enclosed bodies of water along the coast where freshwater from rivers and streams meets and mixes with saltwater from the ocean), and from there, they start migrating upstream.

After entering freshwater, the "glass eels" metamorphose into *elvers*, young eels. They gain their color — usually a brown or gray tone — and grow to be about four inches long. As the eels develop and grow even more, they change to a brownish-yellow color and are then called "yellow eels." During this stage, eels are nocturnal, swimming and feeding at night.

It takes five to twenty years for the eels to mature from when they metamorphose into elvers. When they are finally mature, the eels undergo one last transformation, in preparation for their journey back to the Sargasso Sea to spawn. Their bodies become silvery, their eyes grow larger, they build up fat reserves, and their digestive tracts degenerate, making it impossible for them to eat during their long swim. These "silver eels" travel several months and some 3,000 miles to take part in a mass spawning event — and then they die.

Wacky Fact:

Moray eels have the ability to tie their bodies into knots! They use this ability to gain leverage when tearing food.

Wondrous

Black and White

The zebra moray eel is a mid-sized species of moray eel that is known for its beautiful black and white "zebra" stripes. These eels make their homes in narrow coral caves. Zebra morays hide all day, and then swim out at night to hunt along the crevices of the reef for prey. Their teeth tell the tale of their diet. Unlike most moray eels, the zebra moray eel feeds almost exclusively on crabs, sea urchins, and other hard-shelled prey. While some moray eels have sharp, pointed teeth for grabbing and holding onto their prey, zebra moray eels have flat, plate-like teeth, perfect for crunching on hard shells.

That's Shocking!

Some species of fish look like eels, and are called eels; however, they are not true eels. One example is the electric eel. Despite its name, the electric eel is actually a type of knifefish and is more closely related to the catfish than it is to a real eel.

Electric eels live in freshwater ponds, rivers, and streams in South America, and feed on small fish, frogs, salamanders, and birds. When electric eels attack prey or feel threatened, they are capable of releasing a 600-volt electrical charge. This charge is about five times the amount of power that is in a standard wall socket. The electricity that the electric eel uses to shock its prey is produced in three pairs of organs that are found in its abdomen. These electricity-producing organs, which take up around 80 percent of the eel's body, contain about 6,000 specialized cells called electrocytes. Electrocytes store power in them, much like tiny batteries.

In addition to having this unique ability to release electrical charges, the electric eel is also known for its unusual breeding behavior. In the dry season, a male electric eel makes a nest from its saliva, into which the female electric eel lays her eggs. As many as 17,000 young electric eels will hatch from the eggs of one nest!

Did You Know?

The shock of an electric eel has been known to knock a horse off its feet!

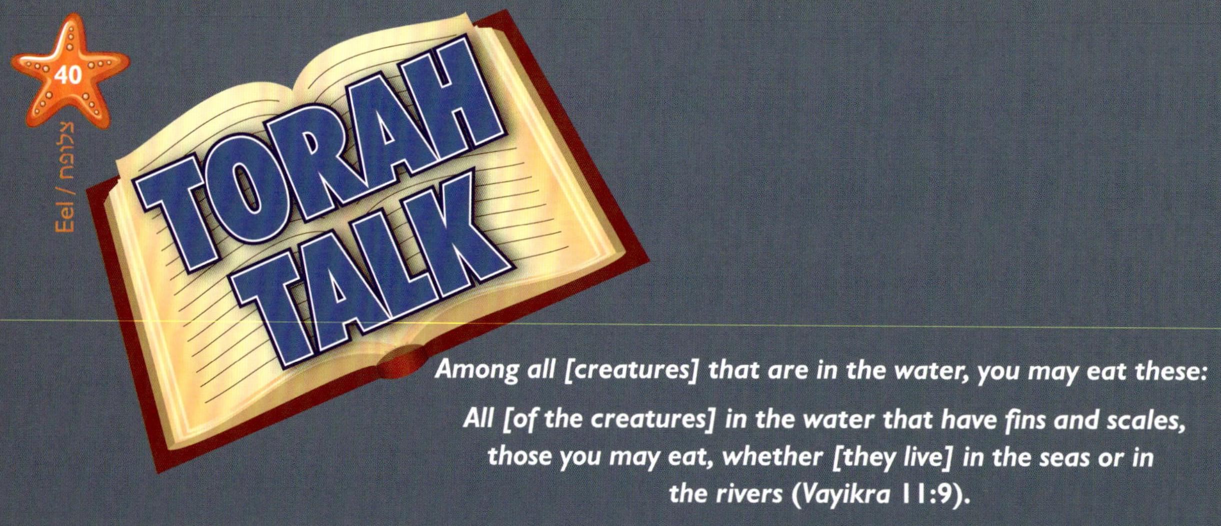

Among all [creatures] that are in the water, you may eat these: All [of the creatures] in the water that have fins and scales, those you may eat, whether [they live] in the seas or in the rivers (Vayikra 11:9).

Fish must have two signs in order to be permissible for our consumption: fins and scales. The Torah states clearly that if either sign is missing, the fish is impure and unfit for our consumption. Accordingly, if a piece of fish that has scales but does not have fins was placed on a plate before us, by these rules, we would have to decline eating it. However, since we have not seen the entire fish, we could raise the possibility that maybe the whole fish from which the piece was taken *did* have fins, but the fins were cut off and thrown away.

Chazal come to our aid by telling us: *Any fish that has scales has fins, but there are fish that have fins but no scales* (*Niddah* 51b). As such, we are permitted to eat the piece of fish on our plate, although we see only one of the two required signs — scales but not fins — because we are assured that if the fish has scales, it must have had fins as well.

Today, over 30,000 species of fish have been classified, and not one of them has scales but does not have fins. How did *Chazal* know, in those ancient times, about facts that scientists have only recently discovered? The *mefarshim* on the Gemara (see *Tosafos* on *Chullin* 66b) explain that *Chazal* knew these facts because Hashem Himself, Who created all the fish that exist in the world, revealed this information to them through Moshe at Har Sinai.

Thus, not only have those who wish to refute the words of *Chazal* been unsuccessful, they have been disproven by their own claim. After searching the whole world to find a fish that had scales and no fins, they thought they found a candidate…only to discover that that fish has a fin, as well!

Record Breaker:

On record, the heaviest eel ever captured was a long-finned eel which weighed 98.5 pounds. It was caught in the Clarence River of New Zealand in 1926.

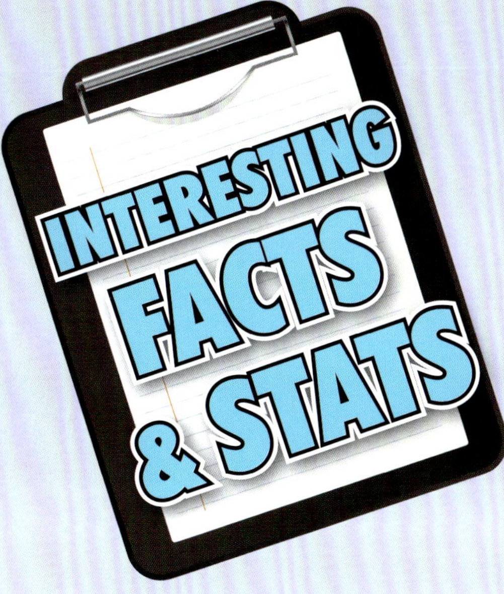

Eels that live deep in the sea are usually gray or black. Eels that live in tropical areas have bright patterns and colors on them.

Garden eels live in burrows on the sea floor. They poke their heads from holes in the sand, while most of their bodies remain hidden. They are called "garden" eels since they live in large groups, and the many eel heads sticking out from the seabed look like plants in a garden.

Over time, the electric eel's eyes are affected by its own electrical discharges. Its eyes develop a hardening of the cornea called a cataract. Eventually, the cataracts cause the electric eel to become blind.

Eels can swim backward as well as forward.

Unlike most other fish, moray eels don't have scales. In order to protect themselves against scrapes and parasites, moray eels ooze a slimy coating of mucus over their bodies.

The moray eel has two jaws! Besides for the usual jaw, there is also a mobile, inner jaw which is lined with razor-edged, hook-like teeth. Situated in the moray eel's pharynx, this "pharyngeal jaw" can thrust forward at lightning speed into the mouth, virtually eliminating any chance a prey might have had at escaping from the first set of jaws.

Eel Trivia

1. An eel is considered to be a…
a. reptile **b.** snake-like amphibian **c.** fish **d.** a, b, and c

2. Young eels are called…
a. eelings **b.** ellettes **c.** elvers **d.** silver eels

3. Which statement is true?
a. Electric eels are not really eels. **b.** Eels have a poor sense of smell.
c. Eels are kosher in Israel. **d.** Eels are unable to live out of water.

4. Why are eels in their second phase of life called "glass eels"?
a. They are fragile. **b.** They are shiny. **c.** They are smooth. **d.** They are transparent.

5. What do eels depend on most when hunting for prey?
a. their quickness **b.** their camouflage **c.** their flexibility **d.** their sense of smell

ANSWERS:
1. c 2. c 3. a 4. d 5. d

Animal Quackers:

Q. Why did the truck driver cross an electric eel with a sponge?

A. Because his truck needed a shock absorber.

SUPER SEAL!

Elephant seals can dive to depths of nearly a mile, stay submerged for hours at a time, and go for months without sleeping.

ELEPHANT SEAL פיל ים

The Elephant Seal

The elephant seal, also known as the sea elephant, is the largest species of seal in the world, with the average male elephant seal growing to around sixteen feet long. The female elephant seals are much smaller than the male elephant seals, growing to an average length of ten feet long.

The elephant seal gets its name from the large proboscis (nose) of the adult male elephant seal, which closely resembles an elephant's trunk. The male elephant seal's proboscis is used to make extremely loud, roaring noises that intimidate intruders. More important, the male elephant seal's long, inflatable snout also acts as a sort of re-breather; it is filled with cavities that are designed to re-absorb moisture from the animal's exhalations. This is necessary, since there are times when the elephant seals are unable to leave the beach for food and water, such as when they must defend their territory on the shore, and they need to conserve vital body moisture as they have no other source of incoming water.

There are two types of elephant seals found in the world's oceans: the northern elephant seals and the southern elephant seals. The northern ones are found in the northern hemisphere, in the Pacific Ocean near the coasts of Mexico, Canada, and the United States. Southern elephant seals live in the southern hemisphere, mainly in sub-Antarctic and Antarctic waters that feature extreme, frigid conditions. A minority of them can also be found on the coasts of Argentina, South Africa, and New Zealand. The southern elephant seals are larger than the northern elephant seals. Southern males can grow to be as large as twenty feet long, and can weigh over 8,000 pounds.

Elephant seals have a thick skin and fur to keep them warm in the freezing cold waters, but it is the thick layer of blubber that elephant seals have under their skin that does the best job at insulating them. Their skin molts every year, although they must return to land in order for the old skin to shed and the new skin to grow.

Elephant seals spend around 80 percent of their lives in the ocean. They are able to hold their breath underwater for over two hours, which is longer than any other water-based mammal. Elephant seals dive to depths of around 1,600 feet to hunt for food, although some have been observed diving to more than 5,000 feet underwater.

Fast Fact:

They may appear to be slow, but elephant seals can move faster than human beings on sand!

Wet, Wild, &

Seafood Diet

Elephant seals spend nine months of the year at sea and are skilled hunters. They often dive thousands of feet beneath the waters in search of prey. It remains a mystery how these creatures are able to hunt for food at such great depths, where there is complete darkness.

Elephant seals have large appetites and eat around forty pounds of food per day. Their favorite foods include: large fish, squid, octopus, eel, and even small sharks. The southern elephant seal has also been known to hunt the smaller species of penguins. Elephant seals usually swallow their prey whole and digest it in about six hours.

Seals of Science

In an effort to learn from the elephant seal's survival methods and lifestyle so that they can be adapted for humans, scientists are studying this animal's behavior by tracking and tagging them with satellite devices. In one study, a video camera was glued onto the back of an elephant seal. Through the study, biologists were hoping to discover a way for children to survive long periods submerged in cold water (as elephant seals live in such conditions); to understand how doctors could control irregular heartbeats (as elephant seals have an irregular heartbeat); and to learn more about sudden infant death syndrome (as elephant seals often stop breathing when they are asleep on land — a condition known as sleep apnea — without it having any negative effects on them).

The tracking devices scientists use on elephant seals also provide information about the currents, temperatures, and salinity in the depths of the southern ocean.

Sealed and Delivered

After an eleven-month pregnancy, the female elephant seal gives birth to a single pup. During its first month of life, the pup feeds solely on its mother's fat-enriched milk and gains about eleven pounds a day. While nursing its young, the mother does not eat and loses one-third of her body weight. The mother nurses until her pup reaches about 300 pounds.

When the pup is two months old, it goes out to sea without any training or instructions. There it must be able to fend for itself. Only one in seven pups reaches four years of age.

Wacky Fact:

Elephant seals often stop breathing for up to half an hour, even while they are on land. They do this in order to conserve energy.

Wondrous

Unique Traits

Elephant seals have a number of unique adaptations which allows them to dive to such great depths: 1) They have a very large volume of blood, twice the amount of any other land mammal their size, which allows them to hold a huge amount of oxygen-carrying red blood cells. 2) They have large, extra spaces in their abdomens called sinuses, which hold blood. 3) They can store oxygen in their muscles. 4) Their heartbeat slows from 55–120 beats per minute to 4–15 beats per minute. 5) They are able to divert the flow of blood from their extremities and restrict it to their vital internal organs.

All of these changes allow the elephant seals to use less oxygen, thus enabling them to dive underwater for such long periods of time and to such great depths.

They're Back!

At one time, elephant seals were aggressively hunted for their blubber, which is a source of oil, and their numbers dwindled almost to the point of extinction. In 1890, there were only about 100 elephant seals remaining in the whole world! Fortunately, its population has rebounded under legal protections. Elephant seals are currently a protected species in the United States and Mexico. Their population has increased over the past 100 years and is continuing to grow at an average annual rate of 6 percent.

Diving and Thriving

Elephant seals are able to dive to incredible depths of over 5,000 feet. These are greater depths than any other aquatic mammal can dive to, including the sperm whale, which can descend deeper than most submarines. The average elephant seal's dive is forty minutes, but some elephant seals stay submerged for two hours (for deep dives, it takes around sixty minutes to descend and about the same amount of time to return to the surface). It is incredible that elephant seals are able to dive continuously, twenty-four hours a day, for months at a time, without sleep. No other mammal can go without sleep for such long periods.

Did You Know?

All elephant seals like to flip sand over themselves when they're ashore. The sand acts as a sunscreen and helps them keep cool.

So long as elephant seals are not disturbed, they are quite placid creatures. Their demeanor changes drastically, however, when their rest is disturbed, or when they are woken from their afternoon nap, which they often enjoy while lying on sheets of ice. When one bumps into another, even if only by accident, the "attacked" elephant seal immediately wakes up and delivers a good smack to its "attacker." This often leads to a serious quarrel between the elephant seals.

Such behavior seems to us strange and irrational. However, before we smile and laugh, we should realize that some people, too, often exhibit this same irritability. They may seem relaxed and easygoing, but all that changes as soon as one approaches them at the wrong time or in the wrong way. No explanation or justification seems to satisfy these irritable people, no matter how good one's intention may have been when approaching them. They always seem to translate things as negative. Any good advice, guidance, or even just a smile, is interpreted as scorn, as an attempt to denigrate or just disturb them. It is awfully difficult to live around such people.

Needless to say, this kind of behavior is not the Torah's way. To the contrary, we are required to improve our characters, so that we become pleasant people and make others feel good. Perhaps the first step to achieving this goal is to judge others favorably. In every potentially negative situation, one should consider all circumstances relevant to the individual with whom he is dealing. Only when one puts himself in the other's place and allows his heart to fill with love and compassion for each Jew can one reach the standard of conduct of "finding favor in the eyes of man and G-d."

Record Breaker:

The largest elephant seal ever measured was 22½ feet in length and weighed four tons. This record has stood since 1913.

INTERESTING FACTS & STATS

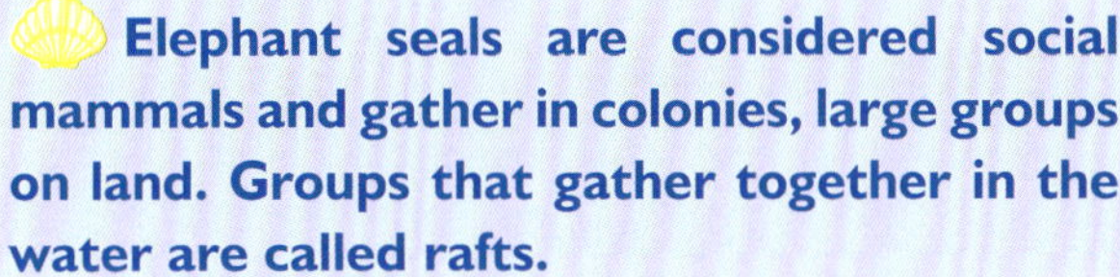

- Elephant seals are considered social mammals and gather in colonies, large groups on land. Groups that gather together in the water are called rafts.
- Elephant seals use their extraordinary diving skills to escape potential predators like great white sharks and to find food sources that few other marine creatures can reach.
- A female elephant seal has an average life expectancy of about twenty-three years, and can give birth once it reaches four years of age.
- Elephant seals can stay on land for longer than any other seal, as they are able to stay dry for several consecutive weeks.
- During its lifetime, the female elephant seal will give birth to up to ten pups.
- The male elephant seal must stay in its territory in order to defend it. This could mean going for months without eating. It survives without food and water by living off of its storage of blubber.
- Elephant seals can swim at estimated speeds of 10–15 mph.
- Elephant seals travel around sixty miles a day en route to their feeding grounds.
- When fighting, elephant seals use their teeth to rake the necks of their opponents.

Elephant Seal Trivia

1. How many different species of elephant seals are there?
a. one **b.** two **c.** three **d.** forty-two

2. Elephant seals are also known as…
a. pinnipeds **b.** sea elephants **c.** walruses **d.** a and b

3. The male elephant seal makes a loud noise with its…
a. tongue **b.** tail **c.** nose **d.** nails

4. Which statement is false?
a. Male elephant seals are much larger than females ones. **b.** Only the males have large snouts.
c. Males are able to stay submerged underwater for longer periods of time than females. **d.** All are false.

5. All elephant seals are…
a. mammals **b.** reptiles **c.** fish **d.** amphibians

ANSWERS: 1. b 2. d 3. c 4. d 5. a

Animal Quackers:

Q. Why did the elephant seal wreck three boats and two ships in one day?

A. Because he went on a crash diet.

FROGS צפרדע

Frogs

Frogs are amazing creatures and among nature's great marvels. They belong in the class of animals called amphibians. These are animals that live both on land and in water.

There are about 5,000 different species of frogs around the world. All adult frogs have the same basic body structure: a stout body, protruding eyes, a cleft tongue, limbs folded underneath them, and the absence of a tail. Frogs are well known for their coiled, sticky tongues, which they project from their mouths to catch insects. These creatures are also well known for being able to breathe through their skin as well as from their lungs.

Frogs are found all over the world, with the exception of the polar regions. Besides living in freshwater and on dry land, some species are adapted to living underground or in trees. In this section, we explore four distinct frogs to help illustrate the diversity of size, color, and behavior between the various species of this creature.

The Horned Frog

Horned frogs have a reputation for being fearless creatures. They have voracious appetites and will attempt to swallow anything that moves close to their wide mouths. They will even attempt to eat things larger than themselves! If threatened by a large animal, the horned frog can deliver a painful bite. It is not afraid to jump toward its attacker, even if the attacker is much bigger than it.

The horned frog is a passive hunter; it remains motionless as it waits for prey to come in its vicinity before attacking. As it is armed with vomerine teeth (teeth on the roof of its mouth, as well as around the outside of its jaw), it is nearly impossible for prey to escape once it is in the horned frog's mouth. The horned frog's typical diet includes insects, small birds and mammals, lizards, and other frogs.

There are two main species of the horned frog: the Argentine horned frog and the Cranwells horned frog, both of which are found in the wetland areas of Argentina, on the tip of South America. The Argentine horned frog is the most common species of the horned frog. (It is also commonly known as the Argentine wide-mouthed frog or the Pacman frog, due to its close resemblance [large mouth and large stomach] to the characters in the Pac-Man video game.)

Female horned frogs are slightly larger than the males. They can be as long as eight inches, and they can weigh up to seventeen ounces. Horned frogs are usually quite colorful. They are bright green, with dark red to black markings all along their backs.

Fast Fact:

Horned frogs are sometimes called "mouths with legs," because their mouths appear to be the entire top half of their bodies. The name "horned frog" comes from the folds of skin that are located above their eyes, which gives the impression of horns.

DANGER!
The golden dart frog has enough toxin in it to kill up to twenty men or about 10,000 mice!
Wacky Fact:
The poison dart frog's brightly colored body actually serves as a warning device to its potential predators that it is extremely toxic.

The Poison Dart Frog

Poison dart frogs are a group of frogs that are native to the tropical jungles of Central and South America. There are over 175 different species of poison dart frogs, and they vary in size, color, and the levels of toxin that they produce. Most species are extremely small. Some, as adults, are less than one inch long, although a few grow up to 2.4 inches in length. Many are brightly colored and come in an array of beautiful color combinations such as yellow, orange, blue, green, black, and red.

Poison dart frogs, also known as dart frogs and poison arrow frogs, excrete toxins through their skin. They are called by these names due to the fact that tribesmen living close to these frogs would use the frogs' poison to help with their hunting, by coating the tips of their arrows and blow-darts with it.

Due to the high toxin levels produced by the poison dart frog, it has very few predators in the wild. Many animals will become extremely sick from just licking a poison dart frog, so they won't approach the frogs at all. There is only one species of snake, *Leimadophis epinephelus*, that is known to be immune to the poison of the poison dart frog.

Poison dart frogs live on the ground or in the foliage just above the ground. They are found in moist and humid forests that are free from high levels of pollution. As carnivorous animals, they survive on a diet purely made up of meat. When hungry, they shoot out their long, sticky tongues to catch flies, ants, insects, spiders, and termites.

The adult frogs lay their eggs in moist places, such as on leaves, in plants, and among exposed roots. Many species of the poison dart frog make devoted parents, as they carry their eggs from ground level, where they were laid, to the safety of the canopy of foliage above. The eggs stick to the mucus found on the back of the mother poison dart frog, while she carries them to a water-pool (a tiny pool made of rainwater) that she locates in a flower high in the trees. The female poison dart frog does this with all of her babies, and lays unfertilized eggs in these water-pools at regular intervals for her young to eat.

Today, many species of poison dart frogs are considered to be critically endangered in the wild, mainly due to pollution and habitat loss.

Did You Know?

Although the secretions from all poison dart frogs are poisonous, only a few species have enough poison in them to kill a human being.

Where'd He Go??

When the red-eyed tree frog closes its eyes, its green eyelids help it to blend in with the leafy surroundings — making it practically invisible.

Fast Fact:

Despite their bright and colorful appearance, red-eyed tree frogs are not venomous.

The Red-Eyed Tree Frog

The tree frog is a small species of frog that spends its life in the trees. True tree frogs are found inhabiting the forests and jungles in the warmer regions all over the world. They are best known for their distinctive, disc-shaped toes at the end of each leg. The rounded toes of the tree frog give its feet more suction and therefore a better grip when it moves around in the trees.

There are four main species of the tree frog. The red-eyed tree frog is the most distinctive of the tree frog species and is native to the jungles of Central America. It has a long, narrow body and hind legs which point outward. While most of its body is a bright shade of green, the red-eyed tree frog is quite colorful, with its bright blue and yellow streaks, large orange toes, and its characteristic bulging red eyes.

Red-eyed tree frogs are carnivorous creatures, feeding primarily on insects, flies, worms, and spiders, which they catch with their long and sticky tongues. Sometimes they will eat other small vertebrates, including other frogs.

Due to its small size — 1.5 to 2.75 inches — the red-eyed tree frog has numerous predators wherever it lives in the world. Birds, mammals, and reptiles of all shapes and sizes prey on red-eyed tree frogs, as well as other kinds of tree frogs, too. Tree frogs are also known to be a tasty treat for large fish.

The red-eyed tree frog is nocturnal. It sleeps by day stuck to the underside of a leaf. While sleeping, it remains camouflaged, as it hides its bright colors by closing its eyes and tucking its feet under its body. When disturbed, the red-eyed tree frog will flash its bulging red eyes and reveal its huge, webbed, orange feet and bright blue and yellow stripes. This technique, called startle coloration, may cause a predator such as a bird or a snake to hesitate momentarily, offering the red-eyed tree frog the opportunity to escape unharmed.

Female red-eyed tree frogs will lay clutches of eggs on the underside of leaves that are standing above a water source. These eggs develop into tadpoles in just a few days when they fall into the water below. The metamorphic process of the tadpoles developing into adult tree frogs can take anywhere from a few weeks to several months.

Wacky Fact:

Red-eyed tree frogs tend to walk and climb, rather than hop and jump. They use the suction cups on their fingers and toes to climb trees and leaves.

WHAT'S FOR DINNER?

Bullfrogs are cannibalistic; they will eat their own kind!

Did You Know?

Unless and until its prey moves, the bullfrog will not recognize it as food. The bullfrog would starve to death if it were surrounded by living but motionless insects.

The Bullfrog

The bullfrog is a medium-sized frog that is best known for its loud, bull-like calls; hence its name. The body of a bullfrog can grow to be around six inches long, not including their legs. Their long legs add another eight to nine inches to its length. Female bullfrogs are usually larger than the males.

The bullfrog is one of the most widely distributed frogs across the North American continent. It is a highly aquatic species, spending most of its life in or near water. It can be found in a wide range of freshwater habitats, including ponds, swamps, and lakes. Bullfrogs like to stay closer to the banks rather than out in the open water. During exceptionally wet weather, they may move away from permanent water bodies.

Bullfrogs are nocturnal; they hide and rest during the day but are very active and hunt for food at night. They are also carnivorous and have enormous appetites; they will eat just about anything! All bullfrogs have huge mouths and very large, sharp teeth which they use to devour their prey. They are ambush hunters that prey on any animal they can overpower and stuff down their throats. Besides the basic frog diet of insects, worms, and small fish, the bullfrog will also eat small mammals, birds, snakes, turtles, mice, and even other frogs.

Because the call of the bullfrog can be heard from long distances, it attracts many different predators. Large fish, turtles, and snakes are its most common predators. When attacked, the bullfrog will attempt to escape by splashing and leaping into deeper water. If trapped, it will let out a loud scream in an attempt to surprise its predator momentarily, giving it time to escape from its clutches. Its loud scream also alerts other bullfrogs of the pending danger, giving them the opportunity to hide or escape to deeper waters.

The female bullfrog can lay up to 25,000 eggs, which float together on the surface of the water. The bullfrog eggs hatch in less than a week, and thousands of bullfrog tadpoles emerge into the surrounding water. Gradually, the tadpoles begin to develop limbs and start to look like adult frogs. This whole process can take anywhere from three months to three years, depending on where the bullfrog lives.

Bullfrogs are generally quite hardy animals and can live up to ten years in the wild. One bullfrog kept in captivity was said to have lived to the age of sixteen!

Fast Fact:

Bullfrogs use their powerful back legs to make great leaps of up to six feet.

Leap of Faith

When Chananiah, Mishael, and Azariah (three Jewish officers in the court of Nevuchadnezar, emperor of Bavel) faced the choice to either bow before an idolatrous image or be thrown into a fiery furnace, they took their lesson from the frogs which plagued Egypt. They reasoned: If the frogs entered the burning ovens of Egypt to carry out the will of Hashem (*Shemos* 7:28), we certainly should be willing to sacrifice ourselves for our Creator.

One of the most remarkable things about those brave and selfless frogs in Egypt was that they jumped into the fire *though they are cold-blooded creatures and by their very nature shun heat and fire.* Yet they overcame their nature in obedience of Hashem's wishes. This is an inspiring lesson for us. How much more so should *we* obey Hashem's commands, especially when we are not called upon to sacrifice our very life but merely to overcome our evil inclinations and temptations!

Importance to Man

Frogs are very useful to man. They are used in scientific experiments to help find cures for diseases, which has helped advance the world of medicine. Frogs also protect our plants by keeping insect populations under control (a cricket frog, for example, eats about 4,800 insects every year).

A Peaceful Ending

The Plague of Frogs seems to have also solved a problem that agitated the Egyptians and the Ethiopians. *Chazal* comment on the verse, *Behold I will smite all the borders with frogs* (*Shemos* 7:27), that a by-product of the Plague of Frogs was the fact that it established peace between the Egyptians and the neighboring Ethiopians. There was a dispute between the Ethiopians and the Egyptians in which each accused the other of encroaching on its borders. When the Plague of Frogs came, the dispute was settled, as the frogs reached only the borders of Egypt, thus creating a clear line of demarcation between the two nations. (*Shemos Rabbah* 10:2)

Wacky Fact:

A frog completely sheds its skin every few weeks. After pulling off the old, dead skin, the frog usually eats it! Bon appetit!

The Majestical Metamorphosis – Life Cycle of the Frog

Frogs begin their lives as tadpoles that are hatched in the water from tiny, jelly-covered eggs. As the frog grows, it moves through various stages in a process known as metamorphosis. The lifecycle of a frog consists of three main stages: egg, tadpole, and adult frog.

Stage 1 – The Egg

The female frog lays thousands of eggs at once. The eggs are surrounded by a jellylike covering that provides nutrients to the developing embryos. The jellylike covering has an awful taste, which protects the eggs from predators until they are ready to hatch. Organs and gills begin to form inside the egg, and the embryo lives off the internal yolk, which supplies it with nutrients, for twenty-one days.

Stage 2 – The Tadpole

After its twenty-one-day development period, the embryo forms into a tiny tadpole. When tadpoles first hatch, they float around in the water until they learn how to swim. Tadpoles in this early stage are considered frog larvae, and they resemble fish with large heads and long tails. When the tadpole first emerges from its shell, it attaches itself to a weed in the water. Unlike frogs, tadpoles cannot survive out of the water. Tadpoles have no lungs; instead, they have gills, which they use to obtain oxygen.

The tadpoles begin the metamorphosis process at around five weeks of age. Throughout metamorphosis, hormones regulate a number of changes in the tadpole. The process starts with the development of the tadpole's hind legs. Afterward, its gills disappear and are replaced by lungs; while this is happening, tadpoles develop the ability to breathe through their skin. Other changes the tadpole undergoes include the development of arms, the widening of its mouth, and the lengthening of its tongue. The tadpole's digestive system also changes, as is necessary for it to be able to consume a carnivorous diet once it becomes an adult frog. The final part of metamorphosis occurs when the tadpole's tail grows into its body.

Once metamorphosis is complete, the tadpole transforms into a froglet. Froglets look like miniature versions of adult frogs, just with small, stubby tails. Froglets must remain in the water until they become full-grown frogs.

Stage 3 – An Adult Frog

At approximately twelve weeks of age, a fully developed adult frog with lungs, legs, and no tail emerges from the water. It is now ready to live on dry land, and in time will lay eggs. Then this whole process will begin once again.

Did You Know?

Frogs don't actually drink water with their mouths; they drink it through their skin. A frog's skin absorbs moisture when it is in the water, so its body gets all of the hydration that it needs.

Our Sages tell us that the Plague of Frogs began with a single large frog that emerged from the river. The Egyptians struck the frog in an attempt to kill it, but to their shock, the frog split into two. The Egyptians then struck those two frogs, and they, too, split into two. (Other *mefarshim* say that when the Egyptians hit the big frog, streams of frogs emerged from its mouth.) The Egyptians kept up their flogging, but all they accomplished was a rapid acceleration of the all-encompassing plague that crippled Egypt.

Let us try and visualize this surreal scenario — Egyptians desperately striking at the frogs again and again, only to see them multiply before their very eyes. We cannot help but marvel at the bizarre behavior of the Egyptians. Why in the world would they continue to flog the frogs when each blow just exacerbated the situation? Couldn't they see that striking the frogs was counterproductive? There can be only one explanation for this: the Egyptians were not thinking rationally. As the frogs multiplied, the demented frenzy of the furious Egyptians drove them to more violent reactions, which caused even more frogs to appear. They were caught in a downward spiral headed for disaster, all because of their anger.

Hashem was sending a message to the Egyptians. The message was simple and straightforward. Just as it was futile and irrational to flog the frogs, so would it be futile and irrational to defy the will of Hashem. Just as anger could cause the Egyptians to take leave of their senses and flog the frogs, so could their inflated egos cause them to scorn the Divine retribution of the Plagues and insist on keeping the Jewish people enslaved. It would be the height of madness to disobey the commands of Hashem. Hashem gave the Egyptians a warning within a warning, but they chose to disregard it and disobey Hashem anyway.

In our own lives, things sometimes do not go our way, no matter how much we try. This may very well be a message to us from Heaven. Sometimes, however, we refuse to acknowledge this fact, and stubbornly continue to bang our heads against brick walls, inflicting grievous damage on ourselves and on others in the process. Only when wisdom prevails and our minds take control of our impulses can we recognize Hashem's hand and look inward for the causes of our misfortune. And when that happens, no matter how our problems are resolved, we will be forever enriched by our newfound closeness to Hashem.

Record Breaker:

In January 2012, researchers discovered the world's smallest known frog, *Paedophryne amanuensis*. It is just .27 to .31 inches long — so small that it can easily sit on a dime!

- Frogs don't have the necessary muscles to chew their food. Instead, they use their eyes to force their food down their throats. This is why it looks like a frog is blinking when it is eating. Its eyes are actually sinking down inside of its skull to push down on the food!
- The wood frog actually freezes in the winter and is revived in the spring. When temperatures fall, the wood frog's body begins to shut down, and its breathing and muscle movements stop. The water in the frog's cells freezes and is replaced with glucose and urea to keep cells from collapsing. When there's a thaw, the frog warms up, its body functions resume, and it hops off like nothing ever happened.
- The glass frog has translucent skin, so you can see its internal organs, bones, and muscles through its skin. You can even observe its heart beating and its stomach digesting food!
- The largest living species of the frog is the Goliath frog. The Goliath frog can grow to lengths of thirteen inches (not including its legs) and can weigh as much as eight pounds!
- A group of frogs is called an army.
- If necessary, frogs will bury themselves in the mud and hibernate in order to survive frigid winters. During hibernation, the frog's bodily functions slow down, and it goes into a semi-conscious state.

Frog Trivia

1. The fear of frogs is called…
a. greenphobia **b.** plaguephobia **c.** amphiphobia **d.** ranidaphobia

2. Which is NOT one of the stages of the frog's metamorphosis?
a. tadpole **b.** froglet **c.** larva **d.** toad

3. A frog is…
a. a reptile **b.** an amphibian **c.** a type of fish **d.** an aquatic mammal

4. Which statement is false?
a. Generally, only male frogs croak. **b.** Frogs can sleep with their eyes open.
c. Frogs use their long tongues to drink water. **d.** Frogs shed skin quite often.

5. Frogs need to live near damp places such as swamps and ponds because…
a. They will die if their skin dries out. **b.** Such areas are free of predators.
c. Their primary source of food is there. **d.** They like to swim.

ANSWERS:
1. d 2. d 3. b 4. c 5. a

Animal Quackers:

Q. Why are frogs always happy?
A. Because they eat whatever bugs them.

1+1=?
A jellyfish does not have a brain!

JELLYFISH מדוזה

The Jellyfish

Jellyfish, also known as jellies and sea jellies, are free-floating sea creatures that have soft, gelatinous bodies and long, stinging tentacles. The body of a jellyfish is most unusual, as it does not consist of an outer shell or any bones or cartilage. Over 95 percent of the jellyfish's body is made up of water.

Most jellyfish are transparent and bell-shaped. The top part of the jellyfish's body is referred to as its "bell." On the underside of the jellyfish's bell-shaped body is an opening that is its mouth. There are over 2,000 different types of jellyfish, and they all vary greatly in their sizes and colors. Some jellyfish are colorless; some are bioluminescent; and some come in gorgeous colors such as pink, blue, yellow, red, and purple. The size of a jellyfish ranges from less than one inch to nearly seven feet long, with tentacles up to 100 feet long or more.

Despite their name, jellyfish are not actually fish; they are plankton. Plankton are organisms that live in the water but have limited swimming powers and are incapable of swimming against the ocean currents. Jellyfish inhabit oceans worldwide and are particularly prominent in coastal areas.

The jellyfish is carnivorous, and despite its blob-like appearance, it is a remarkably efficient predator. It has many tentacles that vary in length, depending on the species. These tentacles are covered in a skin that contains special cells, some that sting, some that grip, and some that stick. The tentacles that hang around the bell of the jellyfish hold the stinging cells. The tentacles that hang around its mouth are called oral arms; these are used to pass food into the jellyfish's mouth.

The main use of the jellyfish's tentacles is to capture prey and defend the jellyfish. Jellyfish stun their prey with their tentacles before grabbing onto their victims and bringing them into their mouths. Some jellyfish stings contain poison, which the jellyfish use to paralyze and kill their prey with before eating them. Jellyfish prey on small fish, crabs, tiny plants, and anything else that gets stuck in their tentacles.

The jellyfish's main defense against predators is its transparent body and its sting. Although the jellyfish's sting is a good deterrent against most creatures, some animals that prey on jellyfish aren't affected by the stings. They include sea slugs, ocean sunfish, and sea turtles.

Most jellyfish live less than one year.

Fast Fact:

The uncoiling of the jellyfish's stingers is one of the fastest actions in the animal kingdom. Stingers shoot out even faster than a bullet from a gun!

Wet, Wild, &

Look, Mom – No Hands (or Ears, Nose, or Feet)!

Most jellyfish don't have eyes, ears, a nose, a tongue, hands, or feet. The jellyfish depends on simple sense cells, which are located in ridges along the edge of its bell. These sense cells perform different jobs. Some act as eyes and respond to the sunlight shining on the water's surface. The jellyfish must be able to sense light in order to determine up from down. Other sense cells of the jellyfish act as a nose, sensing chemicals in the water. Still other sense cells enable the jellyfish to keep its balance and guide itself in the water.

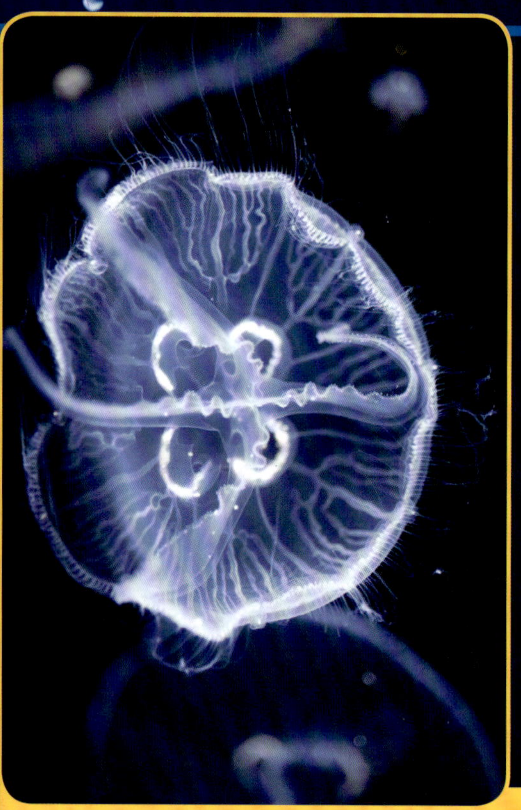

Got a Light?

Some jellyfish, such as the crystal jellyfish, make their own light. They glow or emit flashes of light, either to attract prey or to confuse predators. When lit up, a small jellyfish with long tentacles instantly looks like an intimidating creature. One type of bioluminescent jellyfish drops its glowing tentacles when fleeing from a predator. The predator chases the tentacles, which allows the jellyfish to escape.

Additionally, it has been discovered that the crystal jellyfish can be instrumental in early cancer detection. A process has been developed whereby luminous proteins from the crystal jellyfish can be injected into human cells. Once these cells have been illuminated, a special camera can then detect where the tumors are located in the person's body. Remarkable!

Sting Is Their Thing

Each jellyfish tentacle is covered with thousands of small stinging cells called nematocysts. Inside each *nematocyst* is a hollow tube which looks like a coiled thread. When a creature brushes against the jellyfish, pressure inside the nematocyst causes the thread to uncoil and it injects toxin into the creature through the hollow tube.

It should be noted that jellyfish do not purposely sting humans; most stings occur when people touch a jellyfish. However, the jellyfish's sting can be very painful to humans, and sometimes very dangerous.

Wacky Fact:

Even a dead jellyfish can sting!

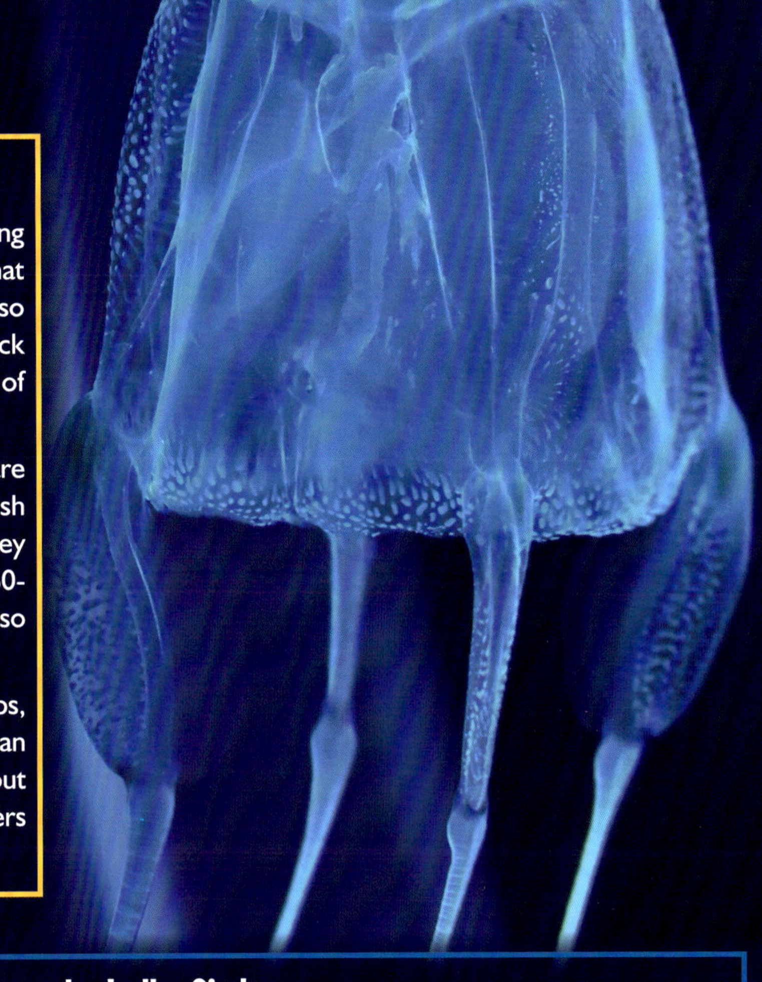

Deadliest Jellyfish

The venom of the box jellyfish is considered to be among the deadliest venoms in the world, containing toxins that attack the heart, nervous system, and skin cells. It is so deadly that people have been known to go into shock and drown or die of heart failure within three minutes of getting stung.

Box jellies, named for their four-sided square shape, are unique among jellyfish in several ways. While most jellyfish do not have any eyes, they have twenty-four eyes! They are from the few animals in the world that have a 360-degree view of their surroundings. Box jellyfish are also able to swim, not just drift like other jellyfish.

Box jellies, also known as marine stingers and sea wasps, are pale blue in color and transparent. Their tentacles can reach up to ten feet in length, and each tentacle has about 5,000 stinging cells. They live primarily in the coastal waters off Northern Australia and throughout the Indo-Pacific.

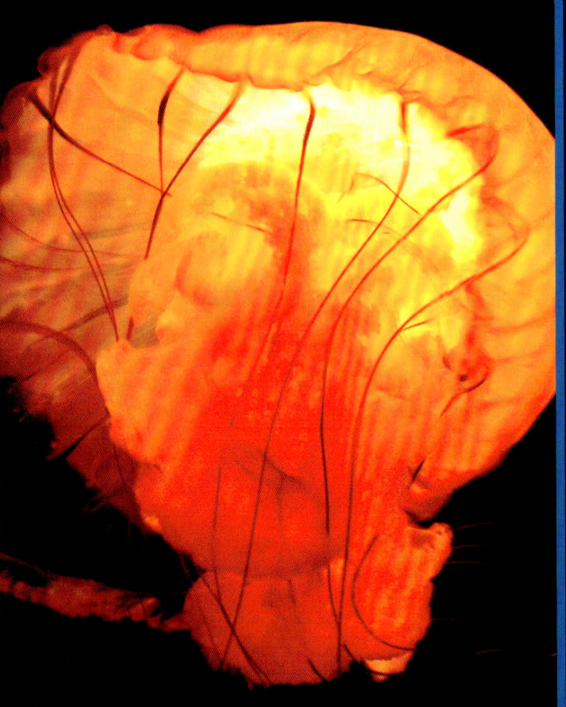

Largest Jellyfish

The lion's mane jellyfish is the world's largest jellyfish. Its bells are over seven feet in diameter, and its tentacles are over 100 feet long. This jellyfish is named for its shaggy oral arms and thin, hair-like tentacles that resemble a lion's mane. The lion's mane jellyfish has eight groups of tentacles, with up to 150 tentacles per group. The bell of its body is pointed, like a star. Lion's mane jellyfish are found in a variety of colors, including red, purple, orange, and tan.

The lion's mane jellyfish eats other plankton, small fish, crustaceans, and even other jellyfish. When hunting for prey, it will lower itself down in the water and spread its long tentacles out like a huge fishing net over its prey.

The lion's mane jellyfish is commonly known to divers for its painful sting. Though the sting is painful, it is not deadly for humans; however, it is toxic and can cause critical burns. The lion's mane jellyfish can be found in the cold waters of the Atlantic and Pacific oceans. The largest lion's mane jellyfish are found in the Arctic Ocean.

Did You Know?

More people are killed by jellyfish each year than by sharks.

Jellyfish are known for their stings. It's an automatic reflex. When a person, fish, or any sea creature comes in contact with it, the jellyfish releases its toxin.

Here's something to think about: why doesn't a jellyfish sting itself? When its long tentacles touch a part of its own body, why doesn't it release any toxin? The answer is that the jellyfish senses a sugar-protein mixture on its body and "recognizes" that it's part of itself — and so it doesn't sting. But without this sugar-protein on itself — without this "sweetness" — the jellyfish would certainly hurt its own body.

In fact, there's a cream on the market that helps protect people from jellyfish stings. The cream contains a mixture of sugar and protein that is similar to the substance found in the jellyfish bell. When the jellyfish comes into contact with this creamy substance, it "thinks" that it is touching itself instead of a person, and so it refrains from stinging.

What a tremendous lesson for us!

We humans can also release a toxic sting, with our tongues; it's called *lashon hara*. Our tongues can be more lethal than the tentacles of the jellyfish. Even a little sting — one negative word — really hurts, and it can have a long-lasting effect.

One reason why it is so easy to talk negatively about others is because we tend to focus on people's shortcomings. However, when it comes to ourselves, we only see and feel "sweetness," like the jellyfish, which is why we would never want anything negative spoken about us.

But unlike the jellyfish, we were not created with an automatic stinging reflex, and so we can actually do something about this problem. Let's work on finding the sweetness in every person, the same way we always try finding the sweetness in ourselves! When we do that, it will become so much easier to stop speaking *lashon hara* about others.

Record Breaker:

The largest jellyfish on record was an Arctic lion's mane jellyfish that was found washed up on the shore of Massachusetts Bay in 1870. Its bell had a diameter of seven feet six inches, and its tentacles reached 120 feet.

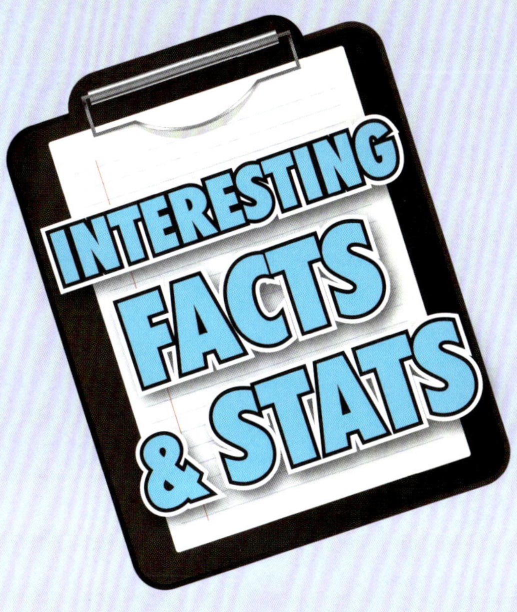

If a jellyfish washes up on the beach, it will mostly disappear as the water evaporates.

A group of jellyfish is called a bloom, swarm, or smack. As many as 100,000 jellyfish can be in one group.

A large bloom of jellyfish was responsible for temporarily shutting down a nuclear power plant in Japan, after the jellyfish became stuck in the plant's cooling system.

Jellyfish digest their food quickly. They wouldn't be able to float if they had to carry large amounts of undigested food around.

The venom in a single box jellyfish can kill up to sixty people.

Jellyfish do not have respiratory systems, since their skin is thin enough that their bodies are oxygenated by diffusion.

The Portuguese man-of-war is not a jellyfish, although it resembles one. In fact, it is not even a single animal. It is a siphonophore, which is an animal made up of a colony of organisms that work together. Specifically, the man-of-war consists of four separate polyps. The top polyp is a gas-filled bladder that reminded people of the sails on a once-common ship called "man-of-war," which is how this creature got its name.

A jellyfish tentacle can sting even if it is separated from the jellyfish's body.

Jellyfish Trivia

1. A jellyfish is mostly made of...
a. jelly **b.** air **c.** blood **d.** water

2. Which one of these body parts does a jellyfish possess?
a. brain **b.** central nervous system **c.** heart **d.** none of these

3. Jellyfish are considered to be...
a. specialized fish **b.** plankton **c.** crustaceans **d.** none of these

4. What is the average lifespan of a jellyfish?
a. three to twelve months **b.** fourteen to twenty-two months **c.** two to three years **d.** twenty-five years

5. Where is the mouth of the jellyfish located?
a. at the bottom of its tentacles **b.** on top of its bell **c.** on the underside of its bell **d.** It does not have a mouth.

ANSWERS:
1. d 2. d 3. b 4. a 5. c

Animal Quackers:

Q. What did the crab say to the fish when it got caught in the jellyfish's tentacles?

A. Help, I'm in a jam!

Born Free
Due to its size, there are very few manta rays in captivity.

MANTA RAY מאנטה ריי

The Manta Ray

There are over 200 different species of rays that inhabit our oceans. Rays are cartilaginous fish, meaning that their bodies are supported with cartilage instead of bone. All rays have a flattened shape, with large pectoral fins fused to their bodies and heads. The manta ray is the largest species of rays and is one of the biggest fish in the sea.

The underside of the manta ray is mostly white, while its upper surface is dark colored. Surface colors vary but are usually shades of black, blue, gray, or brown. The manta ray's body has a disc-like shape, with huge fins that look like triangular "wings" on its sides, and outward, flap-like lobes (called *cephalic fins*) on each side of its head. It uses these lobes to direct food into its huge mouth. The manta ray also has five gill slits on each side of the underside of its body, and a whip-like tail that is slender and slightly flattened.

The manta ray can be easily identified by its tremendous size and grace. It can weigh as much as 3,000 pounds, and it measures between eighteen and twenty-nine feet from wing tip to wing tip. Despite its great size, though, the manta ray is an incredibly graceful swimmer. It is quite breathtaking to watch the manta ray as it glides through the waters. It swims rather fast, but with elegance and seemingly little effort. The movement of its fins through the water is very similar to that of a bird flapping its wings. Another amazing sight to see is a breaching (leaping) manta ray. The manta ray is quite the acrobat; it will occasionally leap completely out of the water and even do a backflip in midair!

One would think that this huge fish would be quite ferocious, but this is not the case. The manta ray has a relatively docile nature and is a rather harmless filter feeder, taking in water and food through its mouth. As it swims, it sieves the food particles out of the water using rows of tiny plates in its mouth. The manta ray feeds on microscopic, planktonic organisms, small fish, and crustaceans.

The manta ray is most commonly found in the warmer, tropical waters of the world's oceans. While it is known to swim quite deep, it is most commonly spotted in shallow waters, close to coral reefs, where it feeds on plankton. The manta ray does not have many predators, but it is preyed upon by large species of sharks, such as the great white shark, and killer whales.

The average lifespan of the manta ray in the wild is twenty years.

Fast Fact:

The manta ray's skin is protected with a mucous membrane that prevents viruses and infections from entering the body.

Migrating Mantas

Manta rays are known to migrate throughout the oceans of the world in search of plankton-rich waters. Some manta rays need to travel hundreds of miles across entire oceans to satisfy their appetite. They also migrate due to the changes of water temperatures that occur during certain times of the year, as they always prefer to inhabit warmer waters.

While manta rays are mostly solitary creatures, during certain migration times of the year, they will travel in large groups. One of the most famous examples of this can be found in Hanifaru Bay, located in the Baa Atoll in the Maldives. Once a year, during the monsoon season, manta rays gather in large numbers to take advantage of the abundant amount of plankton that sweep into Hanifaru Bay. As many as 200 manta rays can be seen at the same time, sweeping back and forth across the bay in dramatic feeding chains. This behavior is sometimes referred to as a "manta ray feeding aggregation." The Maldives is known for the world's largest aggregations of such nature.

Pit Stop

Manta rays frequently need to visit "cleaning stations" to allow small fish, such as wrasse and angelfish, to remove parasites from their bodies. These "cleaning stations" are usually located at prominent coral reefs. The small fish pass through the manta ray's gills and over its skin to feed, in the process ridding the manta's body of dead skin and irritating parasites. Manta rays must have this done on a regular basis.

When there are several mantas at a "cleaning station" at one time, they will form a single line and wait their turn to be cleaned. The manta ray unfurls its cephalic fins and opens its mouth wide, allowing the small fish, its "cleaners," to search and clean its body thoroughly.

Wacky Fact:

The manta ray does not have a nose!

Baby Rays

Most female manta rays only give birth once every two to five years, and usually to a single pup, although on occasion they will give birth to twins. The newborn pup can weigh up to twenty-five pounds at birth, and its fins have a "wingspan" of up to seven feet. The baby manta ray grows rapidly and will double in size during its first year of life. To avoid predators, it spends a considerable amount of time on the bottom of the sea floor. Additionally, it uses its pectoral fins to toss sand over its flat body to avoid being discovered by predators.

Manta Ray Versus the Stingray

Stingrays are probably the most recognized type of ray. There are about 200 species of the stingray, while there are only two species of the manta ray. It is pretty easy to tell the difference between a stingray and a manta ray. The most obvious difference is their size. The manta ray is much bigger and heavier than the stingray. Stingrays range in sizes of one and a half feet to seven feet, while manta rays can grow up to twenty-nine feet.

Of course, the most identifying trait of the stingray is its elongated, thin tail with its barbed stings. Most stingrays' tails have venom glands, which inject an incredibly painful toxin when the sting is used. The manta ray's tail is smaller, and it is not barbed.

A Stingray

Manta One and Manta Two

Until recently, manta rays were considered to be of a single species. In 2009, however, it was discovered that there are actually two distinct species of mantas: the giant manta ray (*Birostris*) and the reef manta ray (*Alfredi*). The giant manta ray is the larger and more widely distributed of the two species. It is more commonly found off shore and is believed to be more migratory.

Although the reef manta ray is smaller, it does grow up to eighteen feet long, and is found closer to shore. The reef manta tends to inhabit the same area all year round, though short, seasonal migrations do occur.

Did You Know?

The manta ray is closely related to the shark.

The manta ray is a large fish, with a large appetite to match. It spends most of its day finding plankton, and consumes up to sixty pounds of food a day. The way the manta ray catches its prey is quite remarkable. It is able to filter the plankton out of the water using a complex system of traps, filters, and gill combs. The manta ray's front fins, called cephalic fins, can be rolled and unrolled during feeding. Unlike many rays, mantas have terminal mouths, meaning that their mouths are positioned at the very front of their heads, between the cephalic fins. When the cephalic fins are unrolled, they help funnel the plankton-filled water into the manta ray's mouth. The food is kept inside the manta's mouth by small plates that are part of the manta's gills. The food sticks to these plates instead of being flushed out of the ray's body together with the excess water. When the manta ray is done eating, it will roll up its cephalic fins and close its mouth. Like that it can swim at a faster speed.

The way in which the manta ray catches and retains its food, which is only possible due to its unique and creative design, renders this creature — together with all others — as incontrovertible testimony to Hashem's hand in the world. Hashem has granted all His creatures the necessary means for obtaining their sustenance. Although the manta ray cannot speak, its testimony to Hashem's *hashgachah* in the world is loud, clear, and undeniably convincing.

If Hashem granted animals the wherewithal to obtain their sustenance, then certainly He did so for human beings, the crown jewel of Creation. It is strange, therefore, that some people think it is necessary to work an extraordinary amount of hours in order to be successful. We must understand that this is not the case at all. True, we must put forth our necessary *hishtadlus* into earning a living, but at that point, we can and should leave it all up to Hashem.

One must constantly bear in mind the words of Dovid Hamelech: *When you will eat the fruit of the labor of your hands, you will be happy, and it will be good with you* (*Tehillim* 128:2). The stress here is on the word *hands*. One should not invest his entire being into the attainment of a livelihood. Rather, one must work for a living only through the appropriate means, leaving his head, the most important aspect of his existence, focused upon Torah study and mitzvos. After all, if Hashem can sustain the giant manta ray, He can and will surely sustain us.

Record Breaker:

The world record for the largest "wingspan" of a manta ray is thirty feet.

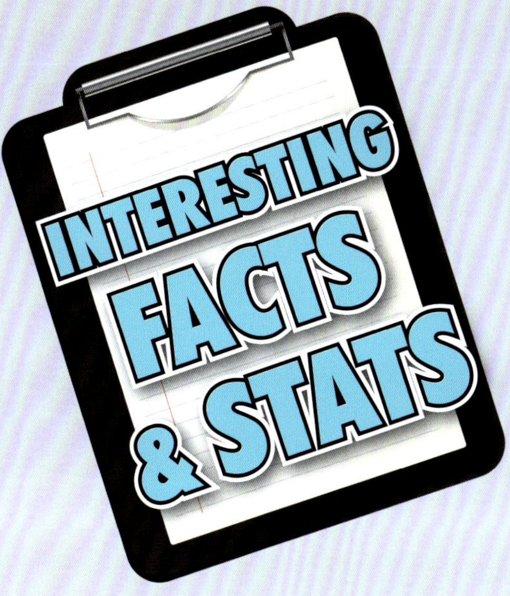

The manta ray is also called the "devil ray," because when rolled and projected forward, the cephalic fins at the front of its head look like horns.

The manta ray can lose its protective mucous membrane if touched by humans.

The manta ray is intelligent and has one of the highest brain-to-body mass ratios of all fish.

The name manta is Spanish for "cloak" or "blanket." One reason why this sea creature was named "manta" is because it looks like a blanket as it moves in the water. Another reason is that there was once a type of a blanket-shaped trap that fisherman used to capture them.

The only marine creatures larger than the manta ray are sharks and whales.

The manta ray is able to perform three different types of leaps out of the water: a forward leap, where it lands head first; a leap where it lands tail first; and an acrobatic somersault flip.

It seems that manta rays are not interested in eating the small fish that clean them — such as the wrasse and the angelfish — because they know that these fish are providing them with a great service.

Unlike other rays, the manta ray does not have a spine on its tail to use for defense.

Manta Ray Trivia

1. How many species of the manta ray are there?
a. one **b.** two **c.** 100 **d.** 200

2. Which creature is the manta ray a close relative of?
a. dolphin **b.** whale **c.** shark **d.** angelfish

3. Which fish helps rid the manta ray of parasites?
a. great white shark **b.** wrasse **c.** plankton **d.** stingray

4. What are baby manta rays called?
a. pups **b.** cloaks **c.** blankies **d.** manties

5. Which statement is false? The manta ray…
a. is a fish **b.** does not have a barbed stinger **c.** is the largest of all rays **d.** gives birth once a year

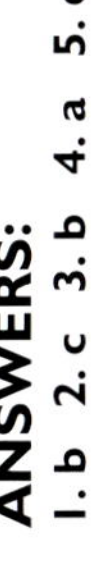

Animal Quackers:

Q. Why did the manta ray cross the ocean during its migration?

A. To get to the other tide.

Give Him a Hand!

If an octopus is caught by one of its arms, it will free itself by breaking off that arm, and a new arm will grow in the missing limb's place!

OCTOPUS תמנון

The Octopus

The octopus is a member of a group of ocean invertebrates (animals with no backbone) called *cephalopods*. Cephalopods are a kind of mollusk, a group of animals that also includes squid and cuttlefish. The name "cephalopod" means "head-foot" in Greek, which refers to the fact that the limbs of these animals are attached to their heads.

There are about 300 different species of the octopus found in oceans all around the world.

Most species live alone in small, rocky crevices or other protected places on the ocean floor. Depending on the species, the size of the octopus varies from two inches to thirty-two feet. All species of the octopus have eight arms, which are usually covered with one or two rows of circular suckers (suction cups) that enable the octopus to cling to surfaces and grasp its prey. Also, the suckers have sensory receptors at the bottom of them, which allow the octopus to "taste" whatever it touches!

The octopus has a highly developed brain and is considered to be the smartest of all invertebrates. In laboratory studies, researchers have observed that the octopus is a highly skilled problem-solver and has the ability to figure out puzzles and mazes. The octopus also has a keen sense of vision and is able to detect colors. This allows it to hunt for prey successfully, even in the deep, dark waters where there is a very low level of light.

Most species of the octopus do not have an internal or an external skeleton. Instead, the octopus's body is made up of a firm but flexible sack of tissues. The only hard part of its body is the beak-like structure around its mouth (similar to that of a parrot), which it uses to tear and bite food. The octopus uses its flexibility to its advantage, both when hunting for prey as well as when hiding from predators; it is able to squeeze itself into amazingly small and tight places and crevices.

Although the octopus can swim pretty fast, its main method of protecting itself against predators is by camouflage. Well known for being a master of disguise, the octopus is able to change its shape, color, and skin texture at the blink of an eye, and while remaining completely still. It will often match its surroundings, blending into the sea floor so well that it appears to be just another rock or even invisible.

Fast Fact:

A fifty-pound octopus can squeeze through a hole only two inches in diameter!

Wet, Wild, &

Now You See It...

The octopus has a most unusual defense mechanism that it uses to protect itself against its predators — the ability to hide in plain sight! Using special pigment cells in its skin, the octopus can instantly change its skin coloring to match the colors, patterns, and even textures of its surroundings.

How does this amazing creature have the ability to blend in with plants, rocks, and even colorful coral in less than a second?

The secret responsible for the octopus's color-changing capabilities lies in its special skin cells called *chromatophores*. Each chromatophore is independently controlled by the nervous system, and each chromatophore consists of three sacs of pigment. By squeezing or expanding these sacs, the octopus can change the color displayed by each cell, allowing it to produce millions of different color combinations. The high level of control by the nervous system is what allows the octopus to change its appearance so fast.

In addition, reflective coatings under the skin cells add to the effect by mirroring the surrounding environment's colors. Projections on the skin called *papillae* enhance the disguise by changing textures, allowing the skin to blend in with surrounding substances such as rocks, sand, or coral.

Octopus hiding among plants and rocks.

Octopus changing colors to blend in with its surroundings.

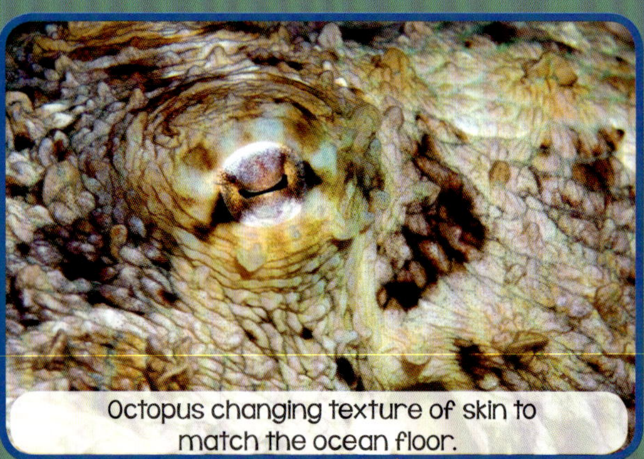
Octopus changing texture of skin to match the ocean floor.

And Now You Don't!

In addition to confusing predators by its color and textural changes, the octopus has another secret weapon in its arsenal — a special substance called ink. The octopus has an ink sac located near its digestive system and, when threatened, will release ink along with a burst of water. The octopus uses this unique weapon in a variety of ways.

If discovered by a predator such as a seal, shark, or whale, the octopus will squirt a cloud of black ink to make the waters dark. This obscures the attacker's view and gives the octopus time to escape. At other times, the inky cloud serves as a decoy. The cloud actually looks like the octopus itself. As the predator attacks the decoy, the real octopus swims away.

Another amazing facet to this ink is that it contains a substance called *tyrosinase*, which dulls a predator's sense of smell and taste. After squirting its ink, besides for having confused its predator, the octopus is now harder to track, and thus it is able to make a quick getaway.

Wacky Fact:

The octopus has three hearts! Two hearts are used to pump blood to each of the octopus's lungs, and the third pumps blood throughout the body.

Small but Deadly

Although all species of the octopus are venomous, only one poses a danger to humans. The blue-ringed octopus, which lives off the southern Australian coast, is only five to seven inches long, and yet it is the deadliest of all octopus; in fact, it is one of the most venomous marine creatures in the world. When it is at rest, the blue-ringed octopus appears gray or beige, with light brown patches, but when it is threatened, its blue rings glow brightly. This warning is usually all that is needed to scare predators away. A bite from a blue-ringed octopus can completely paralyze and kill an adult human in a matter of minutes, and there is no known antidote for it!

Caribbean Reef Octopus

One way to identify a Caribbean reef octopus is by its distinctive dark ring around its eye. The Caribbean reef octopus can be up to sixteen inches long, but when its body is stretched out, it can be up to three feet long. It is fiercely territorial. If another octopus comes by its den, the resident octopus will confront it. If the intruder does not retreat, a vicious fight will ensue. The triumphant octopus usually strangles the other to death and then eats it. At night, when it is ready to rest, the Caribbean reef octopus blocks the opening to its home with rocks, rubble, and shells.

Giant Pacific Octopus

The giant Pacific octopus is the largest octopus species in the world. Each of its eight arms can measure over six feet, and it has an arm span of more than fourteen feet. It is also the longest-living octopus species, with an average lifespan of three to five years. It feeds on small fish, but has been known to attack and eat sharks as well. The female giant Pacific octopus lays eggs only once in her life and is a very protective parent. She can lay up to 100,000 eggs, which she will brood and guard until they hatch. During this period, the mother octopus will not eat. As a result, she dies shortly after her babies hatch.

Did You Know?

The appendages of octopus are called arms, not tentacles. It is a common mistake to refer to an octopus's arms as tentacles. One difference between the two is that tentacles are longer than arms.

One of the most dazzling features of the octopus is, of course, its unique arms. In addition to the octopus's arms' other impressive characteristics, such as their ability to change their length and become longer or shorter as needed, these arms are actually able to grow back if parts of them are ever cut off. The new part of the arm will be identical to the original one that was lost.

Wouldn't it be wonderful if a person had the same ability as the octopus and could grow a new arm or leg if, *chas v'shalom*, he ever lost or was missing the original one, whether due to an injury, sickness, or a birth defect? Then it should be wonderful to realize that we Jews do, in fact, have this very ability, this gift of renewal, albeit in a spiritual sense. By this we refer to the awesome power of *teshuvah*.

A Jew who sins, who does not act in accordance with the Torah, should never despair about his spiritual standing. In His infinite mercy, Hashem grants every person the ability of renewal. Through the process of sincere *teshuvah*, the person can become cleansed of his sin; the "missing parts" of his *neshamah* can "grow back," and he can become revitalized and whole once again.

Record Breaker:

The largest octopus ever recorded was a thirty-foot-long giant Pacific octopus which weighed 600 pounds.

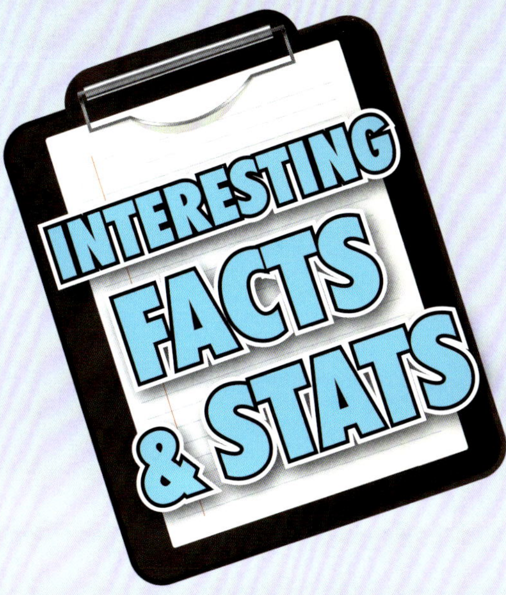

The octopus is among the few creatures that move by means of jet propulsion. Because jet propulsion requires so much energy, many octopus also crawl.

The lifespan of the octopus is generally short. On an average, many species live up to six months. Some of the larger species, however, can live for a few years.

In captivity, the octopus has been known to be able to hide itself in soda cans and aspirin bottles!

The mimic octopus is a species of the octopus that has a variety of capabilities in mimicry. It has been known to imitate many creatures and objects, from giant crabs and seashells to fish and sea snakes.

If cornered in its den or caught by a predator, an octopus will roll into a protective ball by curling all its arms back over its head in order to protect its vital organs.

Researchers have discovered that some species of the octopus reveal their moods through color. For instance, white signals fear, red shows anger, and brown suggests relaxation.

An octopus catches its prey — primarily shellfish and small fish — with its arms. The octopus then bites the prey, injecting it with poison and digestive enzymes. The enzymes partly liquefy the interior organs of the prey, which the octopus then sucks out.

Octopus Trivia

1. The only hard part of the octopus's body is its…
a. beak **b.** mantle **c.** head **d.** nose

2. Chromatophores allow an octopus to…
a. change colors **b.** squirt ink **c.** replace a lost arm **d.** bite its prey

3. The word octopus comes from a Greek word meaning…
a. camouflage **b.** eight-footed **c.** eight lives **d.** sea demon

4. An octopus is a...
a. reptile **b.** fish **c.** cephalopod **d.** amphibian

5. Which statement is false?
a. The octopus can only be found in salt water. **b.** An octopus has eight tentacles.
c. Octopus live in all the oceans. **d.** The octopus is very intelligent.

ANSWERS: 1. a 2. a 3. b 4. c 5. b

Animal Quackers:

Q. Why did the housewife buy a pet octopus?
A. She thought it would be very handy to have around the house.

PENGUINS פינגווין

Penguins

Penguins are aquatic, flightless birds that are highly adapted to life in the water. Famous for their waddling walk and tuxedo-like appearance, penguins typically live on islands or other isolated areas where there is little threat from land predators. Penguins live almost exclusively in the southern hemisphere, in places such as New Zealand, on the southern tips of South America and Africa, and in Antarctica. Despite what many think, penguins are not found only in cold climates; only a few species actually live so far south.

There are about seventeen to twenty different species of penguins. We have selected four very unique species to explore: the Galápagos penguin, which is the only penguin that may be found in the northern hemisphere; the emperor and Adélie penguins, which are found on the ice of Antarctica; and the rockhopper penguin, which compensates for its lack of flying capabilities by jumping.

The Rockhopper Penguin

As its name indicates, the rockhopper penguin actually hops from rock to rock to get about. It is a very small penguin, standing only about twenty inches tall. Despite its small size, it is quite distinguished looking. It sports a decorative crest of spiky yellow and black feathers on its head, blood-red eyes, a red-orange beak, and pink webbed feet.

Rockhoppers are found on islands near Antarctica. Because of their unique way of moving about on land, these penguins are able to inhabit even more extreme environments than other penguin species. In the steep, rocky places where rockhoppers live, hopping from rock to rock is the only way to get around. The rockhopper nests on beaches, high up on the cliffs, and sometimes inland on islands throughout the sub-Antarctic. The rockhopper has no natural land-based predators, since its harsh environment is uninhabitable to other land animals.

During the winter months, rockhoppers spend all their time at sea — they even sleep on the waves. But during breeding season, mass groups of rockhoppers come ashore. These groups, called colonies, consist of hundreds of thousands of penguins. The female rockhopper will lay two eggs, but usually only one survives. The first egg is typically much smaller than the second egg, and it is kicked out of the nest by the parents. Since it is not incubated, it never hatches into a chick.

Both parents take turns incubating the egg that remains in the nest. It can take up to five weeks for the egg to hatch.

The average lifespan of the rockhopper penguin is ten years.

Fast Fact:

Keeping its feet together while hopping, the rockhopper penguin is able to hop up to five feet at a time!

Endangered Species

The Galápagos penguin is the rarest species of penguins in the world. As of 2010, there were only 1,000 pairs of it remaining.

Wacky Fact:

When on land, the Galápagos penguin protects its feet from getting sunburned by holding its flippers over its feet.

The Galápagos Penguin

The Galápagos penguin is the only penguin to live entirely in a tropical climate. True to its name, the Galápagos penguin lives on the Galápagos Islands, which is a large group of volcanic islands located on either side of the equator in the Pacific Ocean. There are eighteen main islands among them, including the islands of Fernandina and Isabela. Since the Galápagos penguin does not migrate, it remains in the area around the islands all of its life.

More than 90 percent of the Galápagos penguin's population lives on the islands of Fernandina and Isabela; the remaining 10 percent is scattered throughout the other islands. Because parts of Isabela lie a few miles north of the equator, the Galápagos penguin has earned the distinction of being the only penguin species that has a population living in the northern hemisphere.

The Galápagos penguin is the third smallest species of penguins in the world and is the smallest of the warm-weather penguins. It stands sixteen to eighteen inches tall and weighs only five pounds. It has a black head with a thin, white band that runs under its chin and a black, upside-down horseshoe shape around its belly. Its beak is longer and narrower than that of other penguins, making it easier for it to hunt for food among the rocks and inside the crevices on the Galápagos Islands.

One of the Galápagos penguin's main problems is keeping itself cool. Close to the equator, where it lives, temperatures reach over 100 degrees during the daytime. One way this penguin stays cool is by swimming and hunting for food in the waters of the Cromwell Current. This current brings cold, nutrient-rich waters to the area, along with a large supply of marine animals, such as krill, squid, and small crustaceans that the Galápagos penguin eats. During the cool nights, the Galápagos penguin will sleep and nest on the land. The volcanic rocks on the islands provide caves and holes for the penguin's nests.

Because of the Galápagos penguin's small size, it has many predators, both in the water and on dry land. On land, it must watch out for crabs, snakes, owls, and hawks, while in the water it must avoid sharks, fur seals, killer whales, and sea lions.

The Galápagos penguin has an average lifespan of fifteen to twenty years in the wild.

Did You Know?

The Galápagos penguins communicate with each other using donkey-like braying sounds.

Up to 50% Off!
The male emperor penguin may lose half of its body weight while incubating its egg.

Wacky Fact:

The emperor penguin may be one of the only species of birds that could spend its entire life without actually walking on dry soil!

The Emperor Penguin

The emperor penguin spends its entire life on the Antarctic ice and in its icy waters. This penguin is the largest of all penguins, averaging about four feet in height and weighing up to ninety pounds. It is also one of the most majestic-looking creatures on Earth. Its most distinguished features are the yellow to orange patches around each side of its neck, as well as the colorful base of its beak. The emperor penguin's head is mostly black, broken up by two large curves that start at the ear and connect to the chest. These curves fade from orange to yellow to white as they move downward from the ears.

Besides being the tallest and heaviest of all penguins, the emperor penguin is also quite unique. Not only is it the only cold-weather penguin that does not migrate during the winter, it even uses the frozen continent as a nursery! During the Antarctic winter, the South Pole becomes the coldest place on the planet. Temperatures fall to minus seventy-six degrees Fahrenheit. The female lays one egg in the winter, in May or early June, and then leaves for two months to forage for food. The female may need to travel fifty miles just to reach the open ocean, where it will feed on fish, squid, and krill. Before leaving, the female transfers the egg to the male. The male penguin rests the egg on its feet to keep it from touching the frozen ground, and covers it with the warm, feathered flap of its skin that's known as the brood pouch. This keeps the egg warm and protected.

In the thick of the winter, the colony of male penguins huddle together to combat the hostile conditions and the 120-mph winds. They take turns moving toward the center of the group, which warms them up. Once a penguin has warmed a bit, it will move back to the perimeter of the group, so that the others could enjoy the protection from the icy elements.

The males stand for about sixty-five days straight, through frigid temperatures, cruel winds, and blinding storms — and they eat nothing the whole time!

The female penguins return to their nests from when the eggs hatch to ten days afterward, from mid-July to early August. They bring with them a belly full of food, and they regurgitate this food for the newly hatched chicks. The males then take off to the sea in search of food for themselves. Afterward, the males return to help raise the chicks. In December, the start of the Antarctic summer, the ice begins to break up, and open water appears, just as the young emperor penguins are ready to swim on their own.

Fast Fact:

The emperor penguin can dive to depths of 1,850 feet for as long as twenty minutes, making it the deepest- and longest-diving bird in the world.

Stop, Thief!
Adélie penguins have been observed stealing rocks from their neighbors' nests.
Did You Know?
French explorer Admiral Durmont d'Urville named the Adélie penguin after his wife, Adèlie.

The Adélie Penguin

The Adélie penguin makes its home on the Antarctic continent and can be found along the Antarctic coastline and on the many small, surrounding coastal islands. The Adélie is among the most southerly distributed of all seabirds, as it is one of only two species of penguins found on the Antarctic mainland (the other species being the emperor penguin). The Adélie penguin is well adapted to life in the frigid Antarctic. It has a thick layer of fat under its skin to help it keep warm, as well as feathers that help keep its body insulated and provide waterproofing for extra protection.

The Adélie penguin is one of the most easily identifiable penguin species, with its blue-black back and completely white chest and belly. Its head and beak are both black, with a distinctive white ring around each eye. Its strong, pink feet are tough and bumpy, with nails that are used for climbing the rocky cliffs to reach its nesting grounds. It also uses its feet when tobogganing across the ice. To toboggan, it slides on its belly, pushing itself forward with its feet.

During the winter months, Adélie penguins migrate north, where they inhabit large platforms of ice and have better access to food. During the warmer summer months, they return south, where they head for the coastal beaches in search of ice-free ground. Once on land, they build nests and line them with small stones. The females usually lay two eggs, one egg a couple of days apart from the other. The male and female take turns incubating the eggs while the other goes off, for up to ten days at a time, to eat. Each chick has an egg tooth, a bump on the top of its beak, which helps the chick break out of its egg. Once the eggs hatch, the parents still take turns looking after their young while the other goes off to gather food.

Like all species of penguins, the Adélie penguin is a highly sociable animal, gathering together in large colonies that consist of thousands of penguins. More than half a million Adélie penguins have formed one of the largest animal colonies in the world on Ross Island, an island formed by the activities of four monstrous volcanoes in the Ross Sea.

The average lifespan of the Adélie penguin is twenty years.

Fast Fact:

Adélie penguins have been known to dive as deep as 575 feet in search of food!

What's for Supper?

Penguins are carnivores, and they are skilled predators. A penguin's vision is its most important hunting tool. Their eyes function better underwater than they do in the air, giving them superior eyesight to find prey while hunting, even in dark or murky waters. Penguins' favorite foods are krill, squid, and fish. Once one of these prey creatures are spotted, the penguin dives into the water and quickly captures it. Then, while still swimming, the penguin swallows its catch whole. Using its prickly tongue and powerful jaws, the penguin is able to maintain a strong grip on even the most slippery of prey.

Purpose of "Porpoising"

Penguins are known to leap in and out of the water in short, shallow arcs when they are traveling at a fast speed, in the same way as dolphins. This is known as "porpoising," and it allows the penguins to breathe without having to slow down. By leaping forward above the water, the penguin is able to inhale air as it swims along. This is necessary when it is swimming long distances. Penguins can be seen leaping over seven feet above the water while porpoising.

Tux and Tails

All penguins have dark backs and white bellies, which gives them a tuxedo-like appearance. Although this look is quite handsome, its real purpose is to serve as camouflage, and it protects the penguins from predators. This unique coloring is called countershading. The penguins' black backs help them blend into the dark ocean bottom, which protects the penguins from predators looking down at them from above. The white plumage on the penguins' bellies looks like the sun reflecting off the surface of the water, which protects the penguins from predators looking up at them from underwater. Not only does the penguins' countershading help them avoid predators, it also allows them to hunt for fish undetected.

Wacky Fact:

Many penguins swallow small stones with their food. The stones make it easier for the penguins to grind their food. Also, it is believed that the extra weight of the stones enable the penguins to dive deeper and for longer amounts of time in the water.

Wondrous

Molting Mania

Penguins molt, or lose their feathers, once a year. They always molt on land or ice, and until they grow new waterproof coats, they are unable to go into the water. Molting is an essential function, as feathers wear out during the year. The new feathers grow under the old ones, pushing them out, but the old feathers do not fall out until the new ones are completely in place.

Penguins do not eat during this period, even though the molting process may take weeks to complete. Before their molt, penguins build a fat layer, which provides them with energy until the molt is over. Most penguins lose about half their body weight during this time.

A molting king penguin

Fluid Fliers

True, penguins cannot fly in the air, but they sure can fly underwater! All penguins are fantastic swimmers and will spend up to 75 percent of their time in water, hunting for food. Their stream-lined bodies, webbed feet, and powerful paddle-like wings, which act as flippers, enable them to "soar" through the water. They can make rapid twists, turns, and loops as they chase after their fast-moving fish prey and escape fast-moving predators. They are unable to breathe underwater, but they are able to stay underwater for ten to fifteen minutes at a time before coming up for air.

Plethora of Penguins

You will rarely see a penguin alone, either on land or in the water. Penguins are very social creatures. They are almost always seen in large groups, as they prefer to live in colonies that number in the thousands. Penguins are constantly interacting with one another, through body language and vocalization. They rely on a variety of sounds to help them identify each other, to warn of danger, and to protect their territory. Some species form a communal nursery group called a crèche. Crèches are guarded by only a few adult birds; this allows the other parents to leave their chicks while foraging for food.

Did You Know?

No penguins live in the North Pole.

There is a basic Torah concept that can be learned from penguins. It's interesting that penguins are such incredibly popular animals. They are among the most popular attractions at all zoo exhibits, along with panda bears and killer whales.

Notice something that these three creatures all have in common? They are all black and white. People are attracted to black-and-white animals because of the bold contrast that they present.

There is a parallel concept to this brought down in the Gemara. The Gemara tells us (*Gittin* 43a): *A person does not properly establish his Torah learning within himself unless he has erred in it.* What this statement is telling us is that information that one acquires quickly and easily does not remain in his mind. To quote a famous expression: Easy come, easy go. Rather, it is the knowledge that comes through laborious effort and through trial and error that is valued by the person and that stays with him for life. It is the very mistakes themselves that the person made that are the cause for his appreciation of the accurate knowledge which he now has.

It says in *Koheles* (2:13): *And I have seen that the advantage of wisdom over foolishness is as the advantage of light over darkness.* This verse is speaking of one who has formerly known only foolishness, but who has now acquired true wisdom. This newfound wisdom will be appreciated by the person far more than it would be by a person who has never known anything different. It is precisely because the wisdom stands in contrast to the person's former foolishness that it is of such great advantage.

This is the same advantage as that of light over darkness. One who has only seen light takes it for granted, but for the one who has known darkness, the light is of infinitely greater value.

We live in a world where there is darkness and evil. But only in such a world can we appreciate light and goodness.

Record Breaker:

The largest penguin colony in the world is on Zavodovski Island, which is an active volcano in the South Sandwich Islands. Approximately 2,000,000 chinstrap penguins breed on the slopes of this island.

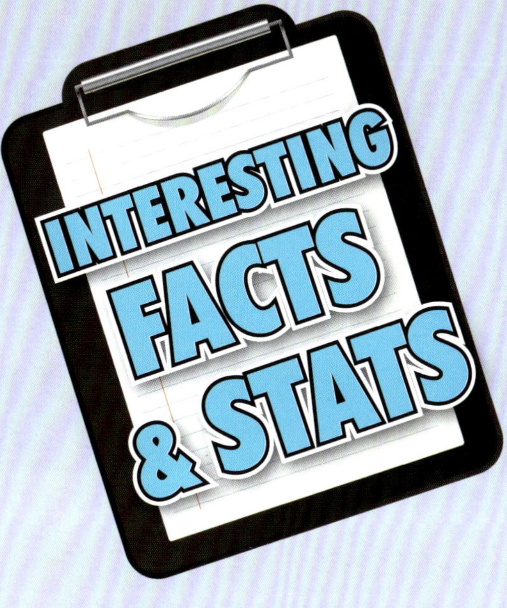

Penguins have more feathers than most other birds, averaging approximately 100 feathers per square inch.

Penguins spend several hours a day preening their feathers. If penguins don't keep their feathers maintained, they will not stay waterproof.

Approximately one in 50,000 penguins is born with brown plumage rather than black. These are called Isabelline penguins. They live shorter lives than other penguins because they are less camouflaged.

The gentoo penguin is the fastest swimming penguin. It swims as fast as 22 mph underwater.

Penguins often toboggan — slide on their bellies over ice and snow. When penguins walk, they waddle in a clumsy way, so tobogganing helps them move quickly while conserving energy.

Penguins usually enter and leave the sea in large groups. Researchers believe that this is for protection, as "there is safety in numbers." By blending into a crowd, an individual penguin may avoid catching the attention of a predator.

Little blue penguins, also known as fairy penguins, are the smallest of all penguins. Their average height is thirteen inches, and they weigh just over two pounds.

Penguin Trivia

1. The largest species of the penguin is the...
a. king penguin **b.** emperor penguin **c.** royal penguin **d.** a and b

2. Penguins are...
a. amphibians **b.** fish **c.** mammals **d.** birds

3. A group of penguins is called a...
a. herd **b.** flock **c.** community **d.** colony

4. A penguin's most effective method of protection from predators is...
a. tobogganing **b.** camouflage **c.** swimming **d.** jumping

5. Which of the following statements is false?
a. Penguins are excellent swimmers. **b.** Male and female penguins look alike.
c. Penguins are not afraid of humans. **d.** There is one species of penguins than can fly.

ANSWERS:
1.b 2.d 3.d 4.b 5.d

Animal Quackers:

Q. Where does a penguin keep its money?

A. In a snow bank!

PIRANHA פיראניא

The Piranha

The piranha is the most ferocious freshwater fish in the world. Known for its sharp teeth and voracious appetite for meat, the piranha will attack any living creature that enters the waters they inhabit, and often eat their own kind. The piranha lives in the rivers of the South American jungles and can be found in nearly every country in South America.

The piranha has a thin body that may be silvery blue, green, brown, or black. It has a large head and a single row of triangle-shaped, razor-sharp teeth in both jaws. It is able to detect blood in the water using the same sensory system as the shark. There are thirty to sixty different species of the piranha, ranging in sizes from five and a half to eighteen inches long.

Despite the carnivorous nature of the piranha, this creature is actually an omnivore. An omnivore will eat almost anything that it can find — either other animals or plants. The piranha usually selects victims smaller than itself, such as fish, snails, insects, and aquatic plants, though it will occasionally eat large mammals and birds that fall into the water. Even attacks on animals as huge as a horse have been documented.

The red-bellied piranha is the most widespread species of the piranha and is the one most responsible for giving the fish its terrifying reputation. Red-bellied piranhas swim in big schools and will attack large fish and any large animal that is in the water. When they attack, a wild feeding frenzy ensues, as hundreds of piranhas converge and pounce on their victim. They use their sharp teeth to chop their prey into tiny pieces. Red-bellied piranhas are also cannibals and will attack and eat other piranhas when other meat sources are scarce.

However, piranhas are not always that deadly, and most species do not even eat meat. In fact, piranhas usually swim alone. Despite its feared nature, the piranha actually has a number of predators in the wild. Piranhas are preyed upon by river dolphins (known as botos), crocodiles, turtles, birds, and larger fish.

The female piranha lays an average of 5,000 eggs at a time. Due to the fact that the male piranha and the female piranha guard the nest so effectively, over 90 percent of the eggs survive, hatching after just a few days. The average lifespan of the piranha is twenty to twenty-five years in the wild.

Fast Fact:

Piranhas will swim from distances of up to two miles to join an attack.

Neither Black nor White – But Red All Over

True to its name, the red-bellied piranha has a reddish belly, and it even has red eyes.

The average size of a red-bellied piranha is six to ten inches long, with a weight of up to two pounds, although some piranhas have been recorded as being as large as twelve inches and weighing eight pounds — yikes! The red-bellied piranha will eat any kind of meat, from insects to fish to animals. Adults hunt at dawn, late afternoon, and night. Young red-bellied piranhas are active mainly during the day — which protects them from being eaten by the adults. Despite the red-bellied piranha's cruel reputation, it is rare for a group of them to attack a person, unless there is blood that it can detect in the water.

Its Bite Is Bigger than Its Bark

The black piranha is one of the most aggressive and probably the most feared of all piranhas. It is quite large; growing up to fifteen inches long and weighing up to eight and a half pounds. The black piranha has been recognized as having the strongest bite among all fish pound for pound, as it can bite with a force thirty times its weight! Its bite strength is nearly three times greater than that of an American alligator of comparable size. The secret to the piranha's powerful bite is its extraordinarily large jaw muscles. In fact, its jaw's muscle complex makes up more than 2 percent of the black piranha's total body mass.

A-Hunting We Will Go...

When hunting for prey, the piranha will use one of two tactics: either it will hide and wait to ambush its prey, or it will aggressively chase after its prey. Adults hunt in groups called *shoals*, which consist of twenty to thirty fish and are led by one or two dominant fish. They usually seek young, ill, or injured victims to prey upon. When food is scarce, however, the group will even attack a large, strong, and healthy adult animal.

The dominant fish of the group finds an animal in the water to attack, and then the other fish in the group join in. Piranhas do not kill their prey before eating it. They use their razor-sharp teeth to tear off pieces of flesh, eating their victim alive.

Wacky Fact:

The piranha secretes a type of mucus, or slime, from its skin. This mucus provides them with protection against infections and parasites.

Wondrous

The President and the Piranha

Although most species of the piranha are not meat eaters, all piranhas are nevertheless thought of as ferocious man-eaters. Believe it or not, the origin of their reputation as vicious creatures was started by a former U.S. president, Theodore Roosevelt.

While visiting Brazil in 1913, President Theodore Roosevelt went on a hunting expedition through the Amazon rainforest. Standing on the bank of the Amazon River, he witnessed a group of piranhas attack a cow with horrifying ferocity. It was a shocking scene: frenzied piranhas, the water foaming with blood, and, within a few minutes, the cow's skeleton floating to the surface of the water. Roosevelt was appalled, and he wrote about his harrowing experience in his 1914 book, *Through the Brazilian Wilderness.*

The following is an excerpt from his book, in which he discusses the piranhas:

They are the most ferocious fish in the world. Even the most formidable fish, the sharks or the barracudas, usually attack things smaller than themselves. But the piranhas habitually attack things much larger than themselves. They will snap a finger off a hand incautiously trailed in the water; they mutilate swimmers — in every river town in Paraguay, there are men who have been thus mutilated; they will rend and devour alive any wounded man or beast; for blood in the water excites them to madness. They will tear wounded wild fowl to pieces; and bite off the tails of big fish as they grow exhausted when fighting after being hooked.

President Theodore Roosevelt on a hunting expedition.

The Rest of the Story...

It turns out, however, that the Brazilians were playing a practical joke on the president. True, President Roosevelt did witness a cow being torn apart by a school of piranhas — but he was totally unaware of the events that preceded his gruesome discovery.

The Brazilians were excited about the president's visit to their country, and they were aware that he had a passion for adventure. In order to impress him, the fishermen blocked off a portion of the river with nets. For days they caught piranhas and dumped them into the river and starved them. The Brazilians told President Roosevelt about these vicious little fish that inhabited their waters and warned him not to go into the Amazon River, or he would risk being attacked and eaten by the piranhas. Naturally, this piqued the president's curiosity, and when he went to investigate, the Brazilians secretly pushed a sick and bleeding cow into the river that was now teeming with starving piranhas. The rest, as they say, is history.

Did You Know?

The word *piranha* means "fish tooth" in indigenous languages of the Amazon. It is a compound word made of the components *pirá*, meaning "fish," and *ranha*, meaning "tooth."

Do fish have to keep the mitzvos and follow halachah? If someone owns a piranha, for example, and it gobbles up a person, is the piranha subject to the death penalty for transgressing the commandment of "thou shall not kill"?

The mishnah in *Bava Kamma* (4:5) states: *If an ox fatally gores a person, the fine levied to the owner depends on the ox's history. If it was a habitual offender, then the owner must pay the fine; if not, he is exempt. In either case, however, the ox must be put to death.*

Although the Torah refers to an "ox" when discussing these *halachos*, the *Chinuch* (mitzvah 52) assures us that these laws hold true for other animals as well. When discussing this halachah, the Rambam (*hilchos nizkei mamon* 10:2) writes, "It is the same whether it is an ox, or any other animal or bird; if it kills a person, it is subject to the death penalty."

Since the Rambam omitted "fish," the implication is that fish are exempt from this punishment. Why should the halachah differ when it comes to the aquatic class?

At this point, it is worthwhile to contemplate the underlying idea behind the halachah to kill a murderous animal. The *Kli Chemdah* (*Parshas Yisro*, sec. 6) refers us to the Gemara (*Shabbos* 146a) which describes the wonderful impact of the revelation at Har Sinai upon its participants.

As a result of the original sin of Adam, all living creatures became infused with a type of spiritual impurity known as *zuhama*. The revelation at Har Sinai had a purifying effect on the Jewish people who were present, cleansing them of their *zuhama*. The *Chiddushei Ha'Ran* (*Shabbos* 108a) explains that this purification process was not limited to the Jewish people; anyone else standing near Har Sinai at the time benefited as well. Thus, the land animals and birds that were standing in proximity to Har Sinai also merited to be cleansed of their spiritual pollution. Fish, on the other hand, were not by Har Sinai.

The *Kli Chemdah* asserts that in light of the above Gemaras, the idea that animals are accountable for their actions is much more palatable. After all, the animals did participate in the revelation at Har Sinai to a certain extent, and they were spiritually affected by it. They were charged with a limited responsibility: namely, don't kill the humans.

With this, the *Kli Chemdah* concludes, we can understand the exemption of fish from the death penalty. Since fish were absent from Har Sinai, they were never charged with the responsibility to avoid human casualty. Therefore, insofar as the death penalty is concerned, the piranha is "off the hook."

Record Breaker:

The largest red-bellied piranha on record was fourteen inches long.

Interesting Facts & Stats

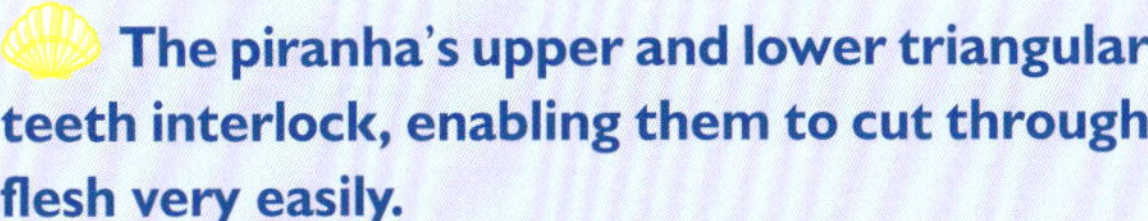

The piranha's upper and lower triangular teeth interlock, enabling them to cut through flesh very easily.

Piranhas and sharks are the only two sea creatures with a heightened sense of smell and an additional sensory system that detects blood.

Young piranhas nibble on the fins and scales of other fish, which provide them with a good source of protein.

One reason why piranhas hunt in groups is to protect themselves from their own predators.

Piranhas are covered in light-reflecting scales, which help to reflect the sunlight and camouflage them in the water to prevent predators from spotting them.

People who live in the Amazon rainforest use piranha teeth as hair clippers!

A school of piranha can contain up to 1,000 fish.

The strong and dominant piranhas tend to stay on the outer edges of the schools, while the young and the females stay protected by swimming in the center of the schools.

Piranhas have a fast metabolism, enabling them to digest their food quickly.

Piranha Trivia

1. A group of piranhas is referred to as a…
a. pack **b.** nursery **c.** shoal **d.** problem

2. If a female piranha lays 5,000 eggs, how many usually survive?
a. under 100 **b.** 1,000 **c.** 2,500 **d.** 4,500

3. A piranha is a type of…
a. dolphin **b.** fish **c.** omnivore **d.** b and c

4. The most common species of the piranha is the…
a. red-bellied piranha **b.** black piranha **c.** white piranha **d.** piraya piranha

5. Piranhas inhabit the waters of…
a. North America **b.** South America **c.** the United States **d.** the Nile River

ANSWERS:
1. c 2. d 3. d 4. a 5. b

Animal Quackers:

Q. Why did the piranha spit out the clownfish it had attacked?

A. Because it tasted funny!

Father of the Year!
The seahorse is one of the only species on Earth in which the male bears the unborn young!

SEAHORSE סוסון ים

The Seahorse

The seahorse is a very unique sea creature. It does not have scales, it does not have a tail fin, and it is not a good swimmer. It does, however, have a long nose, a long tail, and a horse-like appearance — yet this creature is actually a fish!

There are over fifty different species of seahorses. They range in sizes of .6 inches to fourteen inches long. They inhabit shallow, tropical and temperate waters worldwide, with the exception of the polar regions. Seahorses are commonly found around coral reefs, where there is plenty of food and plenty of places to hide from predators.

Although the seahorse does not possess a tail fin, it does have four other fins — one at the base of its tail, one under its belly, and one behind each cheek. Instead of scales, the seahorse has a bone structure that is made up of small, interlocking, bony plates that are covered by a thin layer of skin. These bony plates are arranged in rings throughout the body. Each species has its own distinct number of rings.

The seahorse has numerous distinctive features that enable it to survive in its marine environment. It uses its elongated snout as a vacuum to suck food into its body. Its long, prehensile tail (tail that is able to grasp things) helps the seahorse move through the water, and it also allows the seahorse to anchor itself down by clinging onto coral and aquatic plants. The seahorse moves very slowly, and spends its time bobbing in the sea grasses and coral reefs, sometimes clinging onto the same coral or plant for days. Due to its coloring, the seahorse is able to camouflage itself into the aquatic plants and coral to hide from predators. Some species of seahorses have colors that allow them to blend in perfectly with their coral habitat, while other species have the capability to change colors in order to blend in with their environment.

The seahorse is an omnivore, eating a mixture of plant and animal matter. It feeds primarily on brine shrimp, plankton, tiny fish, and algae. Its small size and lack of mobility are what give the seahorse so many predators within its natural environment. Crustaceans such as crabs, fish, and rays are all common predators. Seahorses are also vulnerable to bad weather. During storms, they are often thrown off their resting places, and they end up being washed up on the shore.

The lifespan of the seahorse ranges from one to six years in the wild.

Fast Fact:

According to *Guinness World Records*, the slowest-moving fish in the world is the dwarf seahorse, which travels at a top speed of about five feet per hour!

Wet, Wild, &

Role Reversal

The seahorse is best known for the remarkable fact that the male seahorse is the one responsible for childbearing, as it is the father, not the mother, that actually carries the eggs before they hatch. The average clutch (group of eggs) size is 100 to 1,000 eggs for most species of seahorses, but it may be as small as just five eggs (for the smaller species) or as large as 2,500 eggs. Once born, baby seahorses are totally on their own. Less than one in a thousand will survive long enough to become an adult, because of their predators.

Eye-Ya-Yaye

Seahorses have excellent eyesight. Their eyes are very intriguing; each one moves independently of the other! The seahorse is able to rotate its eyes 360 degrees, and it can look forward and backward or upward and downward at the same time! Amazingly, the seahorse has the uncanny ability to look for food with one eye while watching for predators with the other eye. So, even though the seahorse does not swim very fast, its unique visionary skills allow it to detect danger early enough to camouflage itself and avoid predators.

S.O.S.

The seahorse is a highly endangered creature, due to habitat loss and overhunting. Habitat loss is caused by coastal development, water pollution, and land-based deforestation. Deforestation leads to increased siltation in surrounding marine waters (siltation is a process by which water becomes dirty as a result of the fine mineral particles that get into it), which kills sea grass beds and destroys coral reefs.

Because of its unique appearance and popularity, the seahorse is hunted to support the high demand in the souvenir and aquarium industry. Another reason why the seahorse is endangered is because it is a popular ingredient in Asian medicine. Millions of seahorses are harvested every year for this purpose alone.

Wacky Fact:

Seahorses have no teeth and no stomach. Food passes through their digestive systems so quickly, they must eat almost constantly in order to stay alive.

Wondrous

Fish Tails

Researchers have discovered an unlikely innovation for armor that may one day be used to protect soldiers and bomb disposal robots — the tail of a seahorse. After extensive tests, researchers have concluded that the seahorse's tail is exceptionally good at protection, as it can be compressed to about half its size before permanent damage occurs. The tail's extraordinary flexibility is due to its structure; it is made up of bony, armored plates that slide past each other. Researchers plan to use a similar flexible material to build a specialized robotic arm that could be used in medical equipment, underwater exploration, and robotic bomb detection and detonation units.

In the past, researchers studied the outer coverings of other animals, such as the armadillo and the crocodile, but this time, when planning this specialized robotic arm, they were specifically seeking an animal covering that would be both flexible and strong enough for this use. When they discovered that the seahorse's tail could be compressed to such a degree without sustaining any lasting damage, they knew they had found the right creature.

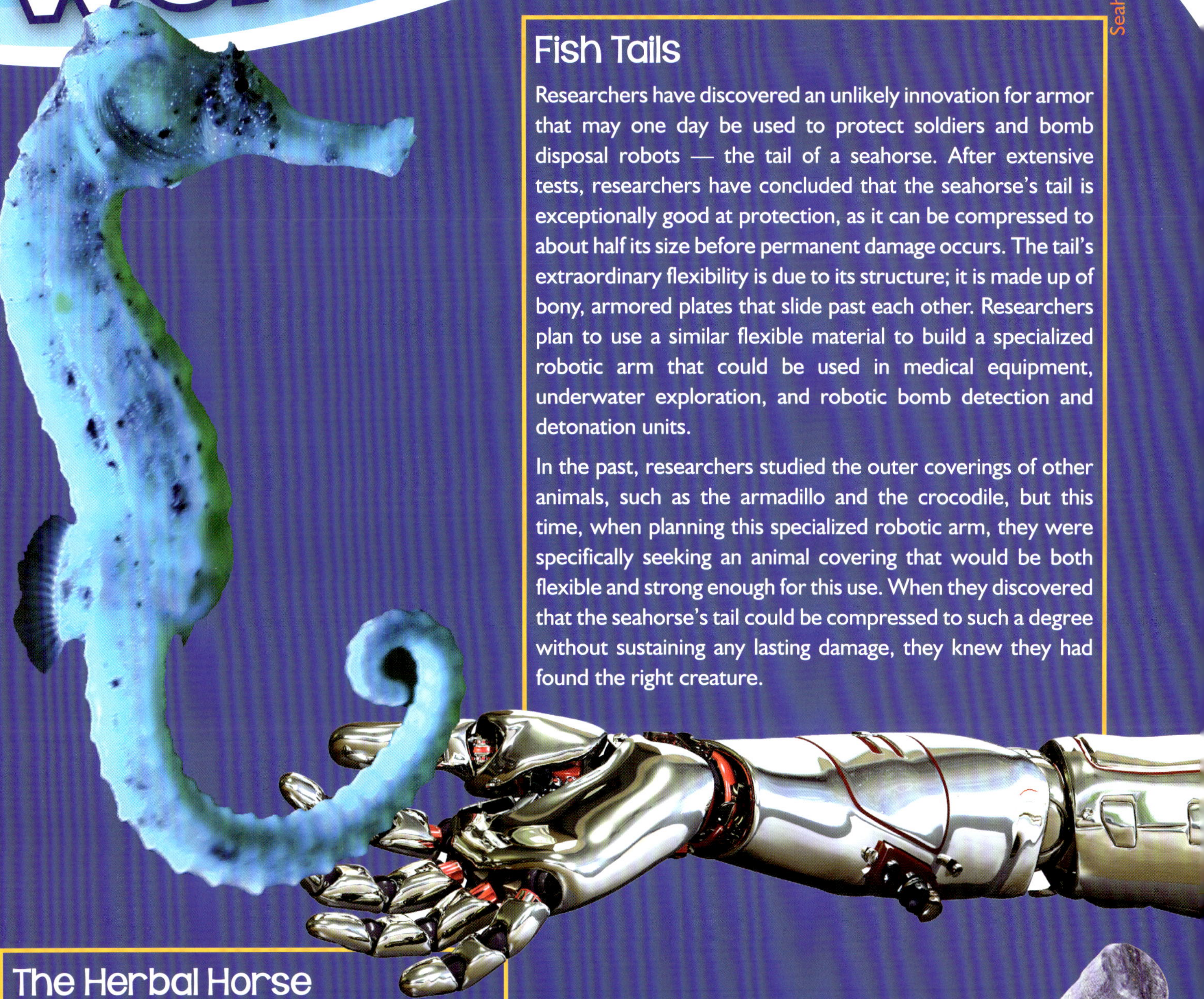

The Herbal Horse

Many Asian nations have been using seahorses for thousands of years as part of an herbal medicine regimen. The seahorses are processed into a fine powder and either mixed into tea or inserted into capsules. The Traditional Chinese Medicine market uses processed seahorses to treat a variety of illnesses, from asthma to arteriosclerosis. Seahorses are also used as remedies for skin ailments, high cholesterol levels, heart disease, lower back pain, insomnia, poor digestion, and lymph node disorders.

Did You Know?

A two-week-old seahorse can consume as many as 3,000 to 4,000 brine shrimps in a day!

The seahorse's head actually resembles that of a horse — hence its name, the "seahorse." It is not the only sea creature to resemble a counterpart living on dry land. There is also the sea lion, the elephant seal, and many others. Indeed, as our Sages teach us, everything which exists on dry land can be found in the seas as well (*Chullin* 127a). This shows us that essentially, there is no difference between the world that exists on dry land and the world that exists underwater.

On land we are privy to an incredibly diverse and beautiful world, with countless species of animals and plant life. Underwater, however, things are no different; if anything, there is an even richer world there, a universe literally teeming with exotic creatures and plants. The only difference between the two "worlds" is that life on dry land is open and visible for all to see, whereas the wondrous life that exists in the waters is more difficult to see and study, as it is hidden from our eyes, covered over by many feet of water.

As individuals, we, too, possess within ourselves the elements of both "revealed" and "hidden." Our body is our revealed side, while our soul is our hidden one. Sometimes we are tempted to live a "double life," thinking that it is possible to conduct our physical lives without it having any effect on our spiritual lives. But the two are intertwined. Whatever we do with our bodies has a profound influence on our souls. Even though our spiritual side is "hidden" and unseen by us or those around us, it is always there, connected to our physical side, and every bit as real as our physicality.

The seahorse's resemblance to a regular horse should remind us that in Judaism, there is no such thing as living a "double life." Our inner self must match our outer self at all times, in accordance with the will of Hashem.

Record Breaker:

The largest seahorse on record was 7¼ inches long.

Interesting Facts & Stats

- The seahorse will use its tail to fight, if necessary.
- The seahorse changes color when it is stressed.
- The male seahorse has a pouch in which it carries its eggs.
- The seahorse uses fins on the sides of its head to help with steering and balance.
- Seahorses are the only fish besides the razorfish that swim vertically.
- The ridges on the top of a seahorse's head, called a *coronet*, form a pattern. This pattern differs from one seahorse to the next.
- Seahorses alone belong to the genus *Hippocampus,* from the Greek words for "horse" (*hippos*) and "sea monster" (*campus*).
- Seahorses can be found in different colors, such as orange, red, yellow, green, and gray.
- Seahorses come in two common patterns, zebra stripes and spots.
- The pygmy seahorse is smaller than one inch long when fully grown.
- Because the seahorse is a poor swimmer, it can die from exhaustion swimming in high currents or storm-tossed waters.

Seahorse Trivia

1. A seahorse is a type of…
a. horse **b.** fish **c.** amphibian **d.** mammal

2. The best way to know if a seahorse is a male is to see if it has…
a. a pouch **b.** an extra fin near its head **c.** a short tail **d.** large eyes

3. Which statement is not accurate?
a. The seahorse has excellent vision. **b.** The seahorse is constantly eating.
c. The seahorse raises its young until they mature. **d.** The seahorse is a poor swimmer.

4. The seahorse primarily uses its tail to…
a. fight **b.** swim **c.** grab **d.** eat

5. Which of the following body parts does a seahorse possess?
a. teeth **b.** stomach **c.** scales **d.** gills

ANSWERS: 1. b 2. a 3. c 4. c 5. d

Animal Quackers:

Q. Why is it usually difficult to hear what a seahorse has to say?

A. Because it is always a little hoarse.

SEA OTTER לוטרת הים

The Sea Otter

The sea otter is the smallest mammal in the marine world and is native to the northern and eastern coasts of the Pacific Ocean. Despite being the smallest aquatic mammal, the sea otter is the largest member of the weasel family. It can reach five feet in length and weigh up to 100 pounds.

The fur of the sea otter can range from brown to almost black, with guard hairs (long, coarse hairs that cover and protect the soft underfur of an animal) that may be black, light brown, or silver. The sea otter has a long, flat tail and webbed hind feet that allow it to swim efficiently in the water — which is vital, since the sea otter spends most of its life in the water. It is even able to close its ears and nostrils in the water, and can live in the water for its entire life, if necessary. But unlike other marine mammals like the whale, which cannot survive on dry land for too long, sea otters are able to walk onto land to rest, groom, or nurse.

Another difference between the sea otter and all other marine mammals is the fact that the sea otter does not have a layer of blubber to keep it warm. Instead, it relies on its dense fur to keep the cold out. The sea otter is known to have one of the thickest, warmest coats of fur in the whole animal kingdom. This coat helps keep the sea otter warm in the cold waters of the North Pacific. Its fur consists of two layers: a waterproof layer of long guard hairs, and a layer of short, thick fur underneath that. Air around the fur is heated by the sea otter's body heat, and this air in turn keeps the sea otter warm.

Sea otters are omnivores, as, aside from eating meat, they do eat seaweed and other aquatic plants. Most sea otters, however, have a primarily carnivorous diet and are known to eat many different species of marine animals. Although the sea otter is a very social creature, it hunts and forages for food alone. It primarily hunts sea urchins, clams, crabs, snails, and small fish in the water. The sea otter mainly stays near the surface of the water, but it will dive as far as 250 feet underwater when hunting for food. The retractable claws on its front paws enable the sea otter to grab and hold onto its prey.

The female sea otter usually gives birth to one pup per year. Mother sea otters will nurse their pups for up to a year, at which time the sea otter pups are able to hunt and forage for food by themselves.

Sea otters can live up to twenty-five years.

Fast Fact:

The sea otter even gives birth in the water. As a matter of fact, the sea otter is the only otter that is able to give birth in the water.

Wet, Wild, &

Tool Time

The sea otter is the only marine mammal in the animal kingdom that has the ability to use tools. For example, the sea otter will use a rock to open a hard-shelled prey such as a clam or a mussel. In order to pry open the shell of its prey, the sea otter places the rock on its chest and then takes its prey and smashes it repeatedly against the rock until the shell breaks open. Keep in mind that all of this is happening while the sea otter is floating on its back in the water! Sea otters always eat in the water and never on land.

Great Groomers

The fur of the sea otter is the finest of any mammal, consisting of 850,000 to 1,000,000 hairs per square inch. These hairs keep the sea otter warm while it is in the water.

Sea otters are meticulously clean. They spend hours each day grooming their coats, which includes cleaning their fur, untangling knots, removing loose hairs, rubbing their fur to squeeze out water, and blowing air into their fur. After eating, they wash themselves in the water frequently, grooming their fur with their teeth and paws. It is extremely important that sea otters keep their fur clean of dirt and debris, in order that it remains waterproof and able to insulate them against the cold. If the fur is covered with dirt or other substances, air cannot penetrate through the fur's hairs, and the sea otter will get too cold.

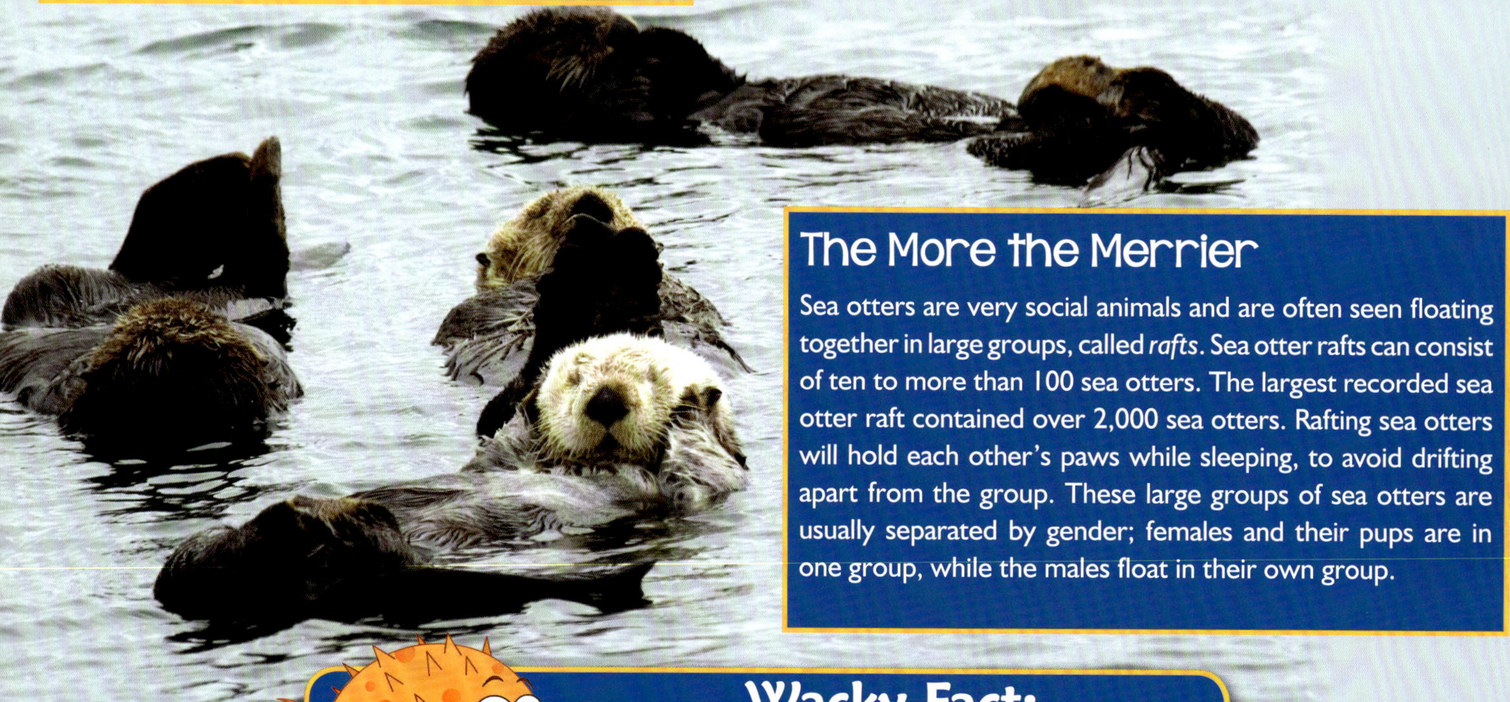

The More the Merrier

Sea otters are very social animals and are often seen floating together in large groups, called *rafts*. Sea otter rafts can consist of ten to more than 100 sea otters. The largest recorded sea otter raft contained over 2,000 sea otters. Rafting sea otters will hold each other's paws while sleeping, to avoid drifting apart from the group. These large groups of sea otters are usually separated by gender; females and their pups are in one group, while the males float in their own group.

Wacky Fact:

A sea otter's coat has pockets, flaps of skin under its forelimbs that it uses to store the food that it catches while hunting underwater.

Sea Otter Versus River Otter

The sea otter and the river otter are related, but they are not the same species of otters. As a matter of fact, there is only one species of the sea otter, while there are around a dozen different species of the river otter. From afar, the river otter and the sea otter may look very similar, but if you know what to look for, you can spot the differences between them rather easily.

• **Watch how they swim.** The river otter swims belly down in the water, while the sea otter swims belly up and floats high in the water.

• **Watch how they walk.** If you see an otter walking easily on land, then it's a river otter. The sea otter does not leave the water often, and when it does, it walks very awkwardly on land, due to its flipper-like hind paws.

• **Watch how they sleep.** The river otter plays in the water by day, but returns to its den on land at night to sleep. The sea otter, though, remains in the water even when it sleeps.

Aqua Pups

The majority of sea otter pups are born in early spring. Newborn sea otters range in weight from three to five pounds. At birth, the pup's eyes are open, it has a full coat of baby fur, and ten teeth are visible. The mother sea otter is a very devoted and nurturing parent, giving her pup constant attention. Besides being responsible for feeding and raising her young, the mother sea otter also grooms her pup to keep its fur clean and cradles the pup to keep it warm. When she needs to dive in the waters to find food for her young, she leaves the pup wrapped and secured in large seaweed.

After a few weeks, the young sea otter should be able to swim, dive, play, groom itself, and eat solid foods. The young sea otter will leave its mother to live on its own between the ages of five to twelve months.

Did You Know?

Sea otters that regularly eat purple sea urchins develop a purple discoloration on their teeth and bones over time.

Although the sea otter has an easygoing disposition and possesses the nicest fur in town, it does not have a carefree life by any means. Actually, *because* of its thick and beautiful fur, the sea otter almost became extinct.

Until the 1700s, sea otters were plentiful, and their population was close to 300,000. But due to a high demand for their fur by the fur trade industry, sea otters' numbers decreased drastically, almost to the point of extinction. Early in the twentieth century, there were only 1,000–2,000 sea otters remaining worldwide. It wasn't until the *International Fur Seal Treaty* was established in 1911 that the hunting of sea otters and fur seals was finally banned. Today, there are close to 150,000 sea otters in existence worldwide. Sea otters are no longer facing extinction, but they are still considered to be an endangered species and are protected by law.

Of course, human hunters are not sea otters' only threat. They must be constantly on the lookout for their two main predators, sharks and killer whales.

Yet interestingly enough, despite all these dangers, and despite it being the smallest marine mammal in the animal kingdom, the sea otter is not a timid creature or one that is easily frightened. To the contrary, it is quite active and ambitious, beginning its day one hour before sunrise each morning to hunt for food.

What a powerful lesson this teaches the person who sees himself as small and thinks to himself, *What am I, and what kind of life is this? Torah study is too difficult, and I have to work so hard to earn a living.* With such a perspective, a person may attempt to free himself from the obligation of studying Torah. Such a person is under the mistaken notion that one is required to learn only when it comes easy, when his mind is clear and without any interfering worries or concerns. This is not the case at all. To the contrary, a Jew receives reward specifically for learning Torah and doing mitzvos in *spite* of the obstacles and difficulties in his way.

We must remember that Hashem, in His infinite mercy, endowed each of His creatures with the strength necessary to achieve his purpose in life. Even when one feels small and alone, Hashem will assist him to successfully deal with any situation, so long as the person demonstrates his willingness to follow the Torah.

Record Breaker:

The deepest recorded dive for a sea otter was 318 feet.

Sometimes the fur on the sea otter's head turns silvery with age. Between its silvery head and its long whiskers, the sea otter is appropriately nicknamed "Old Man of the Sea."

While resting, sea otters keep their feet up, out of the water. This helps conserve body heat. Since sea otters do not have fur on their feet, they would lose heat rapidly if their feet were exposed to the coldness of the water.

The sea otter has a big appetite. It must consume 25-40 percent of its body weight daily, just to keep warm.

While swimming on its back, a sea otter moves at a speed of about 2 mph.

Sea otters can move faster when necessary. They can swim at around 5 mph when chasing prey or escaping from predators.

Sea otters have small front legs and stiff toes for handling food.

Unlike river otters, which can stay submerged underwater for well over five minutes, sea otters can usually stay submerged for only less than two minutes.

It is estimated that more than 2,000 Alaskan sea otters were killed in the Exxon Valdez oil spill in 1989.

The sea otter's long whiskers help it detect vibrations in the dark, murky waters.

Sea Otter Trivia

1. The female sea otter usually gives birth to how many pups per year?
a. one **b.** three **c.** six **d.** twelve

2. Where does the mother sea otter leave her pup when she hunts for food?
a. with the father **b.** with the siblings **c.** with a guardian **d.** wrapped in seaweed

3. Sea otters are the only aquatic mammals that can...
a. swim underwater **b.** live on land **c.** migrate **d.** use tools

4. Groups of sea otters are called...
a. floaters **b.** ottomans **c.** rafts **d.** schools

5. The sea otter is the...
a. largest member of the weasel family **b.** smallest aquatic mammal
c. only otter to give birth in the water **d.** a, b, and c

ANSWERS:
1. a 2. d 3. d 4. c 5. d

Animal Quackers:

Q. Why did the sea otter have trouble getting out of the water?

A. Because it pulled a mussel.

SHARKS כריש

Sharks

Sharks are carnivorous fish that live in waters all over the world. Sharks do not have any bones; instead, their skeletons are made of cartilage and connective tissue. Cartilage is a strong, durable substance that is half the density of bone. It allows for greater flexibility and helps the shark conserve energy. Sharks have an excellent sense of hearing, good eyesight, and a great sense of smell. There are over 400 different species of sharks, ranging in various sizes, from as small as eight inches in length to as large as fifty feet long.

Sharks' diets vary greatly, but all sharks are carnivores and are considered to be top hunters. They will even eat each other if they can't find anything else to eat. In this section, we will be exploring four different species of sharks. Three are the most dangerous sharks in existence, while the other is the largest shark in the world.

The Whale Shark

The whale shark is not only the largest species of sharks, it is the largest fish in the sea. Some adult whale sharks grow to nearly fifty feet long and weigh over fifteen tons! The whale shark has a wide, flat head; a rounded snout; and a huge mouth that can open more than four feet wide.

Despite its enormous size, the whale shark is a gentle giant — a so-called "friendly shark" — as it does not pose a significant threat to humans. Unlike many other species of sharks, the whale shark is known to feed on plankton, krill, and large shoals of tiny fish rather than hunting bigger fish and sea creatures. The whale shark is actually a filter feeder that strains small organisms from the water. It swims with its mouth open and sucks in gallons and gallons of water filled with organisms. After closing its mouth, the shark uses its gill rakers to filter its prey from the water. Gill rakers are bristly structures in the shark's mouth that trap the tiny organisms which the shark then swallows. The remaining water is then discharged through the shark's gill slits.

The whale shark inhabits the warm, tropical waters around the equator. It is known to migrate every spring to the continental shelf of the central west coast of Australia. The coral spawning of the area's Ningaloo Reef provides the whale shark with an abundant supply of plankton.

Whale sharks tend to live for about sixty to eighty years, but some have been known to live longer than that — they can live even more than 100 years!

Fast Fact:

Whale sharks are very slow swimmers, moving along at no more than 3 mph.

Bloodhound of the Sea

The great white shark can detect even the tiniest drops of blood up to three miles away!

Wacky Fact:

When there is a group of great white sharks but only enough food for one of them, the sharks engage in a tail-slapping bout. They swim past each other, each slapping the surface of the water with its tail, directing the spray toward the other sharks. The shark that delivers the most tail slaps gets the meal!

The Great White Shark

The great white shark is the largest predatory fish in the world. It can grow to be as large as twenty feet in length, while weighing over 5,000 pounds. Great whites are found in coastal waters in every major ocean, but are most commonly sighted around Australia, South Africa, California, and Mexico.

The great white is a highly efficient hunter. It has a streamlined, torpedo-shaped body, with a powerful tail that propels it through the water at speeds of fifteen to twenty-five miles per hour. It has an exceptional sense of smell, and it is able to sense the tiny electromagnetic fields generated by its prey. The great white shark's white underbelly (the reason for the shark's name) helps it remain undetected from its prey below, as the whiteness gives the appearance of sunlight shining in from above. Its upper body is a blue-grayish color which blends in with the sea floor, enabling it to remain undetected from prey swimming above it, as well.

When hunting for a meal, the great white will begin its search for prey at the surface of the ocean, while swimming below. Once it tracks down its victim, it swims upward with a burst of speed, bumping into its prey while biting it at the same time. The great white shark can even leap completely out of the water when attacking. It does not chew its food; it tears off chunks of meat and swallows them whole. The great white's mouth is lined with about 300 sharp, triangular-shaped teeth arranged in several rows. These serrated teeth are lethal weapons; a single bite from them can be fatal to its prey. The great white's main prey includes large fish, dolphins, seals, small-toothed whales, and sea turtles.

Although shark attacks on humans are rare, the great white has been known to attack people. Of the 100-plus annual shark attacks on humans worldwide, almost half are attributable to great white sharks. However, great whites do not like to eat or attack humans. Usually, the only time a great white will attack a person is when it mistakes the person for a seal.

The female great white shark usually bears her first young at twelve to fourteen years of age. Once the baby sharks are born, they immediately swim away from their mother. Baby sharks are on their own right from the start. At birth, each baby great white shark is about five feet long already!

Due to the dominance and aggressiveness of the great white shark, it has no natural predators within its regular environment. Its average lifespan is about thirty years.

Did You Know?

More than 70 percent of the people attacked by great white sharks survive, because the shark does not finish its attack once it realizes it has made a mistake and that its victim is a person, not a sea creature.

School's Out!

Hammerheads swim in schools of up to 100 sharks during the day, but they hunt alone at night.

Wacky Fact:

The hammerhead shark is one of the rare animals that can get a suntan! Tanning occurs when hammerheads swim close to the water surface for long periods of time.

The Hammerhead Shark

The hammerhead shark is appropriately named for its flat-shaped head. It mostly preys on large fish, but it will occasionally hunt small water mammals. Hammerheads can be found in the warmer waters of oceans worldwide, but are particularly found in coastal and offshore waters. The shallow water that the hammerhead inhabits allows it to hunt down prey more easily.

The shape of the hammerhead shark's head is made up of two projections on either side of it, which makes it almost rectangular and resembling the shape of a hammer. The eyes and nostrils of the hammerhead shark are found at the ends of the "hammer," which allows the shark to have better senses of vision and smell in the surrounding water. The hammerhead shark's flat-shaped head also helps it detect its prey, by increasing the shark's sensitivity to sonar activity. Hammerhead sharks use sonar wave detection in a similar way to their five main senses, which gives them a sort of "sixth sense." As they swim across the ocean floor, they use their unique heads to scan the sea bed for living creatures they could eat (a lot of their prey hide beneath the sandy floor), in much the same way as a metal detector scans for metal objects.

There are nine different species of hammerhead sharks worldwide, ranging from three feet long to twenty feet long. The great hammerhead shark is the largest species of the hammerheads. It can grow to as long as twenty feet and weigh over 1,000 pounds. Due to its sheer size and its very aggressive temperament, the great hammerhead is potentially dangerous to humans. Other species of hammerhead sharks tend to pose little or no threat to humans, as they are generally much smaller than the great hammerhead shark and are calmer in their nature.

Hammerheads are commonly seen swimming in large groups, called schools, during the summer months, when they migrate together in search of cooler waters. They eat a variety of foods, including small fish, stingrays, small sharks, and squid. They do, however, need to keep an eye out for their own predators. Their main predators are the tiger shark, the great white shark, and the killer whale.

The average lifespan of the hammerhead shark is twenty-five to thirty-five years.

Fast Fact:

Unlike many fish, hammerhead sharks do not lay eggs. The female can give birth to up to forty live pups at a time. The pups are born with soft heads, so the mother is protected while giving birth.

ALOHA!

Large animals such as horses, goats, and sheep are commonly found among the stomach contents of tiger sharks around the coasts of Hawaii.

Did You Know?

The tiger shark is heavily sought after for its fins, skin, and liver. Its liver contains high levels of vitamin A, which is processed into vitamin oil. Due to excessive hunting by humans, the tiger shark is considered to be a near-threatened species.

The Tiger Shark

The tiger shark is the fourth largest shark in the world and is one of the most dangerous predators in the sea. Its name is derived from the stripes it has running down its body, similar to tiger stripes. These stripes, however, are only present in adolescent tiger sharks. As they mature, their stripes start to fade away, and by the time they are adults, the stripes are no longer visible. An adult tiger shark can grow to be more than fifteen feet in length and weigh up to 1,500 pounds.

The tiger shark has a voracious appetite and will devour anything in its path. The stomach contents of captured tiger sharks have included tin cans, license plates, car tires, and even a chicken coop! This shark is extremely aggressive by nature and will stop at nothing to complete its hunt for food. Tiger sharks are of the most dangerous sharks for humans to come into contact with, as they will attack when feeling threatened. The tiger shark is second only to the great white shark in attacking people. However, there is one major difference between the two sharks: because the tiger shark has such a fierce appetite, it will usually not swim away after biting a human, whereas the great white shark frequently will do that.

The tiger shark has sharp, highly serrated teeth and powerful jaws that allow it to crack the shells of sea turtles and large clams. Like most other species of sharks, the tiger shark has sensors on the sides of its head which enable it to detect small muscle movements of nearby creatures. It also has a wedge-shaped head that allows it to turn quickly when necessary.

The tiger shark is a solitary hunter and usually hunts at night, when it is able to move through the water unseen. It usually swims very slowly, which makes it difficult for its prey to detect the oncoming attack. Once the shark is close, a speed burst allows it to reach the targeted victim before the victim has a chance to escape. The tiger shark can reach a top speed of around 20 mph, which is pretty fast in the water!

Tiger sharks can be found in warm and tropical waters in the southern hemisphere. They tend to gravitate to more coastal waters, though they are also known to go into the deeper ocean if they need to hunt for food.

The tiger shark can live up to fifty years in the wild.

Fast Fact:

The tiger shark's reputation as an indiscriminate eater that will consume anything in its path, including garbage, has earned it the nickname: "Wastebasket of the Sea."

The Tooth of the Matter

Sharks may have up to 3,000 teeth at one time. All sharks have numerous rows of teeth. When one tooth is worn down, broken, or lost, it is replaced by another. Most sharks have about five rows of teeth at any time. The front set is the largest and does the majority of the work. Behind the front row of teeth is a second, smaller row of teeth, then a third row, a fourth, and a fifth. When a front tooth falls out, it is replaced by a tooth from the next row. The sets of teeth rotate forward, and a new tooth forms in the rear, sort of like a conveyer belt. Incredibly, sharks never run out of teeth, and they may grow over 20,000 teeth in their lifetime!

Just as sharks come in different shapes and sizes, so, too, shark teeth come in various shapes and sizes. Every tooth is purposely designed to enable the shark to catch and kill its prey. Each type of shark has different shaped teeth, depending on that shark's diet. For example, some sharks have teeth that are very sharp, wide, and jagged (such as the great white, the hammerhead, and the tiger shark). Those kinds of teeth are perfectly designed for catching and tearing apart prey. Other sharks have thin, sharp, knife-like teeth designed to catch and hold slippery fish. Bottom-dwelling sharks have flattened teeth in the backs of their mouths that enable them to crush the shells of crabs and mollusks.

Skin Deep

Unlike most fish, sharks do not have scales. Instead, their skin is covered with tiny, rough, tooth-like structures called denticles. The texture of the shark's skin is similar to sandpaper in its abrasiveness.

The denticles' streamlined shapes help decrease the friction of the water flowing along the shark's body, enabling the shark to swim more quickly while using less energy. The denticles also add protection to the shark; since the shark's skin is so rough, mere contact with it can injure potential predators. Interestingly, the denticles do not grow as the shark grows; instead, they fall off and are replaced by larger ones!

Wacky Fact:

Two of the smallest species of sharks, the lantern shark and the pygmy shark (both around eight inches long), can do something that no other shark can do: they glow in the dark! They are able to make their bellies light up — which they rely upon for camouflage (the light obscures the shark's shadow, camouflaging it against the sunlight filtering down from the surface above) and when hunting in the dark depths of the ocean.

Wondrous

That Makes Sense

One reason why sharks are such successful predators is because they have such super senses. Two-thirds of a shark's brain is dedicated to its sharpest sense: that of smell. Sharks are able to detect certain chemicals in the waters with a concentration as low as one part per billion! Sharks also have outstanding senses of hearing and vision, but most unusual is the shark's sense of electricity and vibrations in the water.

Sharks are able to feel vibrations in the water using a line of canals that go from their heads to their tails. Called a "lateral line," these canals are filled with water and contain sensory cells with hairs growing out of them. The hairs move when the water vibrates, alerting the shark to potential prey. If that wasn't enough, sharks also have a sensory organ called the *ampullae of Lorenzini*, which they use to "feel" the electrical field coming from their prey. All living creatures give off an electrical impulse, either with the beat of their heart, muscle movements, or with their brain. The shark is able to detect these impulses even when its prey hides beneath the ocean floor.

A Shark Is Born

Baby sharks, called pups, are born with a full set of teeth and are ready to take care of themselves. Immediately after birth, pups leave their mothers.

Depending on the species, there are three different ways that sharks are born:

1. The mother shark gives birth to live sharks. This is in much the same way as mammals give birth. Examples of sharks born in this way are the whale shark and the hammerhead shark.

2. The mother shark lays eggs. The eggs are laid in well-hidden areas and will hatch into baby sharks later.

3. Eggs develop inside the mother shark. The eggs hatch and develop inside the mother's body and are nourished by the yolk of the egg and fluids from the mother. Then the pups are born alive. Examples of sharks born in this way are the great white shark and the tiger shark.

Sharks can have one to one hundred babies at a time. The sharks that give birth to live pups have fewer babies at a time than sharks that lay eggs.

Did You Know?

"Galeophobia" means the excessive fear of sharks. It comes from the Greek word *galeos*, which is a particular type of shark.

The tiger shark and the great white shark are two prime examples of apex predators. An apex predator is a carnivore that kills and eats other animals and has no natural predators of its own in its environment. It sits on top of the food chain and has little fear of falling prey to another animal. These sharks are "eating machines," gobbling up everything in their paths, with an appetite that knows no bounds.

However, the most striking thing about the lifestyle of these fearsome predators is their constant activity. They swim and swim and swim, circling around and around in the water, with an unending energy and unceasing motion. The great white shark actually *needs* to constantly swim in order to survive. It does not have the ability to pump water over its gills like most fish, and thus must be constantly swimming in order to breathe; as so long as it keeps swimming, water keeps moving over its gills, providing it with oxygen and thus keeping it alive.

We know that Hashem created every living creature for a reason. We can learn great lessons from everything in the world. What valuable message can we glean from the extreme predatory nature and the continuous movement of these ferocious sharks?

The shark's predatory nature and its restlessness can represent evil and wickedness. Evil and a lack of rest are linked together, as only through Torah and mitzvos can true peace be attained. Without Torah and mitzvos, the soul is in a constant state of searching, as it fruitlessly attempts to fill the void within it with materialism and other mundanities — when all the *neshamah* really wants and needs is spirituality. In *Sefer Yeshayahu* (48:22 and 57:20) it is written: *"There is no peace," says Hashem, "for the wicked..." The wicked are like the troubled sea, which cannot rest.*

In contrast to this sorry state of wickedness and constant turmoil is the day of Shabbos, a day of holiness and of rest. The spiritual nature of Shabbos is what gives it that special quality of *menuchah*. May we all merit to experience Shabbos properly, and be granted the true serenity that emanates from its spiritual goodness, by dedicating ourselves each week anew to Hashem and the Torah and mitzvos.

Record Breaker:

In 1986 a great white shark weighing 3,427 pounds was caught, setting a new world record for the world's largest fish ever caught with a rod and reel.

INTERESTING FACTS & STATS

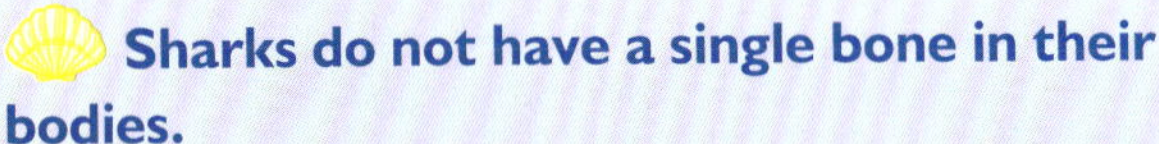

- Sharks do not have a single bone in their bodies.
- Instead of closing its eyelids, a great white shark rolls its eyes into the back of its head when it attacks. This behavior helps the shark protect its eyes from debris and the thrashing of its prey.
- Sharks do not have ears on the outside of their body, but rather on the inside of their heads.
- Sharks only use their noses for smelling, not for breathing.
- The blue shark is a migratory species. It journeys up to 1,700 miles while making its seasonal migration from New York to Brazil.
- Unlike most animals, sharks can move both their upper and lower jaws. A shark can temporarily dislocate its jaw and jut it forward to take a bite out of its prey.
- The mako shark is the fastest of all sharks. It is capable of reaching speeds of 60 mph. It is also able to leap up to thirty feet in the air!
- A shark is unable to eat a small fish called the Moses sole fish. When a shark bites this creature, the creature releases a chemical into the shark's mouth that makes the shark release the fish. Scientists are trying to duplicate this chemical so they can develop a shark repellent.

Shark Trivia

1. What are baby sharks called?
a. sharkettes **b.** pups **c.** guppies **d.** kits

2. Which is the largest species of sharks?
a. great white shark **b.** bull shark **c.** elephant shark **d.** whale shark

3. What are shark skeletons made of?
a. cartilage **b.** small bones **c.** hair **d.** keratin

4. Which shark swims in a group by day but hunts alone at night?
a. tiger shark **b.** ghost shark **c.** hammerhead shark **d.** blue shark

5. Which shark swims the fastest?
a. whale shark **b.** great white shark **c.** mako shark **d.** pygmy shark

ANSWERS:
1. b 2. d 3. a 4. c 5. c

Animal Quackers:

Q. Why did the fish laugh at the man who was screaming, "Help, shark, help!"?

A. Because it knew that the shark was not going to help him.

SNAIL חילזון

The Snail

The snail is a gastropod, a soft-bodied type of mollusk, whose body is protected by a hard shell. It is a slow-moving creature that is only a few inches long and usually weighs just a few ounces. There are over 1,000 different species of snails found worldwide, and they are divided into three groups. There are land snails, sea snails, and freshwater snails.

An adult snail is quite the distinctive creature, due to its unique, hard, coiled outer shell. Snail shells come in various shapes and sizes. The shell is large enough for the snail to retract its entire body into it for protection when it feels threatened. A snail will also go into its shell when the weather is very hot and dry; this helps to keep its moist body from drying out.

Snails have tentacles on their heads. Some species have one set of tentacles, while others have two sets. The snail's eyes are usually located on its longer set of tentacles (if it has two sets). The smaller pair of tentacles is used for the sense of smell and the sense of touch.

Believe it or not, the snail has a foot! Located under the snail's body, this "foot" is actually a long, muscular organ. The snail is able to move by contracting and expanding this muscle.

Snails are generally herbivores, primarily eating vegetation such as leaves, stems, and flowers. Some larger snail species, however, are known to be predatory, either being omnivorous, or, in some cases, fully carnivorous.

In order to break down their food, most snails have thousands of microscopic, tooth-like structures located on their ribbon-like tongue, which is called a *radula*. The radula works like a file, ripping the snail's food into small pieces for the hungry creature.

Due to their relatively small size and slow-paced movement, snails are preyed upon by numerous animal species all around the world. Rodents, birds, fish, and amphibians such as frogs and toads are some of the snail's main predators.

The average lifespan of a snail is approximately fifteen years. However, it is believed that some species live up to twenty-five years, depending on their habitat. In captivity, snails can live longer, due to their needs always being met and the fact that they are also protected from various types of predators.

Fast Fact:

The common garden snail is the slowest-moving animal; it can travel at about 0.03 mph.

Tale of the Snail

Land snails and water-dwelling snails lay eggs. The land snail digs a small hole in the ground and, in just a few days, lays up to 100 eggs inside of the hole. The snail covers the eggs with dirt and slime, and two to four weeks later, the eggs begin to hatch.

Baby snails are born with a shell, but the shell is fragile, soft, and transparent. Snails need calcium to harden their shells, and so the first thing a newly hatched snail does is consume the shell of the very egg it hatched from, in order to absorb calcium from it. In general, baby snails have large appetites and will devour whatever is nearby. Some will even eat the other eggs (its siblings) that have not hatched yet.

The snail's shell continues to grow with it over the course of its life.

Water-dwelling snails lay their eggs at the bottom of the ocean floor. Some lay several thousand eggs within a period of a few days. However, survival is difficult for both land snails and water-dwelling snails. Most are killed by predators before they reach the age of one year.

The Shell Maker

Like most mollusks, the snail has a very important organ called a *mantle*. The mantle is a fleshy tissue which forms the outer wall of the snail's body and lines the inside of the shell, and it's what is responsible for making the actual shell by releasing a substance called calcium carbonate. Over time, the mantle secretes more and more calcium carbonate, which increases the size of the shell.

Sorry – We're CLOSED

When a snail feels threatened, it will curl up inside of its shell. Since the snail is very slow and is unable to fight off large predators such as rodents, birds, or frogs, this is its way of defending itself. In order to remain protected, the snail will seal off the opening of its shell, either by placing the hard part of its foot over the opening or by spreading a layer of hardened mucus over it. Once the shell is sealed shut, the snail is safe from most predators. It can stay sealed up like this for days or even weeks.

Wacky Fact:

As a snail crawls along, it secretes a slimy fluid. This slime coats the ground under the snail, which helps the snail move more easily. The slime also provides a form of suction for the snail, enabling it to cling to things and crawl upside down.

Wondrous

Giant African Land Snail

The giant African land snail is the largest species of snails found on land, with a height of around three inches and a length that can exceed eight inches. It is native to the forest areas of East Africa, but has been introduced into Asia, the Caribbean, and a number of islands in both the Pacific and the Indian oceans. Large colonies of giant African land snails can be formed from just one snail, as it lays around six clutches of eggs every year, with an average of 200 eggs per clutch. In contrast to other kinds of snail hatchlings, around 90% of giant African land snail hatchlings survive, which can cause a previously snail-free area to quickly become infested.

Giant African Land Snail

The giant African land snail is generally seen as a pest, as it will eat almost anything vegetarian that it can find and has proven to be quite destructive when around crops and wildflowers. Giant African land snails are also known to carry parasites that can cause diseases in humans. Because they cause so much damage in such a short period of time, possession of the giant African snail is illegal in some countries, including the United States.

Killer Snails

Cone snails are among the most venomous creatures on earth. There are three different types of cone snails, and they are all venomous. Cone snails that hunt and eat fish are classified as *piscivores*. This type of cone snail uses its *proboscis* to attack its prey. The proboscis is a long, tubular duct that is often several times the length of the snail itself. The snail's proboscis contains a toxin-laced "harpoon" (which is actually a hollow, spear-like tooth), which is attached by a "thread" to the snail, sort of like a fishing line. When the proboscis makes contact with the fish, it injects its harpoon-like tooth into the fish, immediately immobilizing it. Within seconds after being injected, the fish is paralyzed, and the snail reels in its meal.

The venom of some of the larger species of cone snails is powerful enough to kill a human being. Attacks on humans, however, only occur when a cone snail is either stepped on or picked up from the water or the beach.

Cone Snail

Did You Know?

During periods of drought, the giant African land snail goes into aestivation (summer sleep). The snail seals itself inside its shell to retain water. The shell is impenetrable, so the snail will not lose any water during this period.

When the Torah commands the Jewish people to wear *tzitzis*, it tells us to put on the corner of the *tzitzis* a thread of *techeiles* (*Bamidbar* 15:38). The *pasuk* says that this *techeiles* is meant to remind us of all the mitzvos of Hashem.

But what is *techeiles*, and where does it come from? *Techeiles* is the sky-blue dye that was used in the curtains of the Mishkan and in the clothing of the *kohen gadol*.

The Gemara tells us that *techeiles* comes from a sea creature called the *chilazon*, and many sources give us clues as to what kind of animal this *chilazon* is:

It is found between the cities of Tzor and Haifa (*Shabbos* 26a).

It has a shell that grows with it (*Shir Hashirim Rabbah* 4:23).

It looks like the sea (*Menachos* 44a).

It lasts in its beauty (meaning, the dye does not fade or wash out) (Rambam, *hilchos tzitzis* 2:1).

Since *techeiles* was so precious, after *Churban Bayis Sheini*, the Roman emperors forbade anyone but the royal family from wearing or even owning it. For over a thousand years Jews could not wear *techeiles* and wore only white strings on their *tzitzis*. Slowly but surely, knowledge of the dyeing process and the identity of the *chilazon* was forgotten.

Now, after years of research and new discoveries, there are those who believe that the *chilazon* is a snail that lives in the Mediterranean Sea, called the *Murex trunculus*. This snail fits many of the descriptions found in the Gemara, and is known to have been used for dyeing thousands of years ago. Archeologists have recently found Murex shells in Yerushalayim dating from the times of the Beis Hamikdash, which further supports the belief that this type of snail is the *chilazon*.

In ancient times, dyers would catch these snails by putting chunks of meat in baskets as bait and lowering them to the sea floor. The snails would fall for the bait, and the dyers would bring them up from the sea and crack them open. The dyers would then remove from each snail a small gland that was part of the creature's digestive system. When these glands were exposed to air and sunlight, they produced a beautiful and lasting, sky-blue dye.

Since the evidence pointing to the fact that the Murex snail is the *chilazon* is quite strong, today many people do, in fact, wear *techeiles* strings on their *tzitzis*, using the dye of the Murex. However, most people do not do so. This is because they feel that we are still missing something known as a *mesorah* for it, and without a *mesorah*, there is always the possibility that we may be wrong in our understandings. When Mashiach comes, he will clarify this issue for us. We hope and pray that that will be speedily and in our days, amen.

Record Breaker:

The largest land snail ever recorded was a giant African land snail that weighed two pounds and was fifteen inches long.

- There are thousands of species of snails. The only creature that outnumbers the snail is the insect.
- Snails are very strong and can lift up to ten times their own body weight.
- Snails are nocturnal; most of their movements take place at night.
- A snail shell can be rounded, spiraled to a high point, or it can be flat.
- The geographic cone is the most venomous of the 500 known cone snail species, and several human deaths have been attributed to them.
- By studying cone snail venom, researchers produced a painkiller that is 100 times more potent than any existing pain medication on the market.
- A sea snail's eyes stay in one place, but those of a land snail can move from side to side and up and down.
- Many people confuse slugs with snails but they aren't in the same category, as slugs don't have shells.
- The giant African land snail is known to eat at least 500 different types of plants.

Snail Trivia

1. How many different species of snails are there?
a. 3 **b.** 10 **c.** 100 **d.** over 1,000

2. Which part of the snail makes the snail's shell?
a. proboscis **b.** mantle **c.** tentacles **d.** foot

3. What percentage of giant African land snails survive their first year?
a. 90% **b.** 75% **c.** 50% **d.** Most do not survive their first year.

4. Which snail is illegal to own in the United States?
a. sea snail **b.** geographic cone snail **c.** giant African land snail **d.** none

5. Where are the eyes of the snail located?
a. by its mantle **b.** by its foot **c.** on its tentacles **d.** The snail does not have eyes.

ANSWERS: 1. d 2. b 3. a 4. c 5. c

Animal Quackers:

Q. Why did the snail cross the road?

A. I'll let you know when it gets there.

Brainiac
The squid has a very large brain and is extremely intelligent.

SQUID דיונון

The Squid

The squid is a marine cephalopod that is often mistaken for an octopus. While the squid and octopus are similar in some ways, they are two different types of sea creatures. There are around 300 different species of squid found in the oceans worldwide. The squid is one of the few creatures that can inhabit the freezing waters of the Antarctic. Squid habitats are most commonly found in the deepest zones of the oceans. Because of this, most marine biologists believe that there are many more species of squid that have yet to be discovered.

The squid has eight arms and two feeding tentacles, which are longer than the arms. Some species of squid are known to have ten arms! The squid is an invertebrate (animal without a backbone) that has an extremely soft body. Most squid have a long, tube-shaped body, with a large head, a sharp beak, two large eyes, and two lateral fins. The squid has gills which it uses for breathing, so it does not need to come to the surface for air. The size of a squid varies from area to area. Some species are as small as one inch, while others can exceed forty feet in length!

All squid are carnivorous; however, their diets vary according to their size. Smaller species of squid eat krill, plankton, crustaceans, and small fish. Larger species will eat large fish and smaller species of squid, while the giant squid will even eat young sharks and whales! When hunting for prey, the squid usually waits in hiding until its victim is in striking range. Once its prey is in reach, the squid quickly grabs it with its two long feeding tentacles. Then it uses its arms to transfer the prey from its tentacles to its mouth. The squid uses its parrot-like beak to tear off small pieces of its prey so that it can swallow them.

Due to the squid's very soft body texture, it is easy to be consumed and is therefore a common food source for many sea creatures. The smaller species of squid are the ones that are often eaten by small and medium-sized predators. Predators include fish, seals, penguins, sharks, whales, and other squid.

Generally, squid in the wild will only reach up to three years of age before being eaten. Some of the larger species of squid, however, have been known to reach the age of fifteen.

Fast Fact:

The colossal squid, along with its cousin, the giant squid, have the largest eyes in the animal kingdom. Each eye is the size of a basketball!

Mollusks, Start Your Engines...

The squid is the fastest swimming invertebrate in the sea. When necessary (such as when chasing prey or escaping from predators), and for short periods of time, it is able to swim with powerful bursts of speed. In order to accelerate its speed, the squid squirts water rapidly from its mantle cavity (the mantle looks as if it is a hat that protects the main part of the squid's body). The squid moves by jet propulsion: as the mantle opens, water is taken in; and as the mantle closes, water is released through the siphon, a nozzle-like structure located below the eyes. The siphon acts as a jet engine, enabling the squid to "fly" through the waters. The squid shoots backward, tail first, and can propel itself as much as twenty-five body lengths in a second! Some squid even leap above the water and glide over the surface, like flying fish, when being pursued by predators.

The Squid Versus the Octopus

Many people mistakenly think that the squid and the octopus are the same creatures. Although they are both multi-armed mollusks, they have many differences and are easy to tell apart. Below are some of their differences:

- Most squid have at least ten limbs — eight arms and two tentacles. The octopus, on the other hand, has eight limbs — eight arms, and they don't have tentacles.
- The squid has two fins, whereas the octopus has none.
- The squid's body is cigar-shaped, while the octopus has a bell-shaped body.
- Squid use their two feeding tentacles to grab and capture prey, whereas octopus inject venom into their prey, which paralyzes the prey.

Octopus

Very Sensible

The squid makes good use of a variety of senses. It is very sensitive to touch, as well as to taste. It is believed that the squid's tasting ability is about 1,000 times stronger than that of humans. The squid also has a good sense of smell. Additionally, the squid has excellent vision and is able to see in shallow waters as well as deep waters, both during the day and night.

Wacky Fact:

More than $100,000 was paid in December 2005 by the Melbourne Aquarium in Australia for a block of ice that contained the preserved body of a giant squid.

Wondrous

GIANT and COLOSSAL

The colossal squid is not only the largest species of the squid, it is also the largest invertebrate in the world (the giant squid is the second largest). It is quite massive, growing to a length of over forty feet and often weighing over 1,000 pounds.

The colossal squid inhabits the cold waters of Antarctica, New Zealand, and even some areas of Africa. It lives in the deeper regions of the sea, making it difficult for scientists to observe and learn more about them. Adult colossal squid descend to depths greater than 7,000 feet. Most of what we know about these humongous creatures comes from the exploration of their dead bodies that sometimes wash up on beaches.

Besides for being so large, the colossal squid is quite powerful as well. Its size, weight, power, and arsenal of "weapons" make it easy for it to capture large fish to eat. These "weapons" are part of the colossal squid's body, and they are lethal to the squid's prey. Like most squid, the colossal squid has eight arms and two tentacles. What makes the colossal squid unique is that its tentacles possess two rows of sharp, rotating hooks that swivel, as well as two rows of suckers. The arms have more and much larger suckers, and hooks that do not rotate. The colossal squid also has a very large beak, the largest of any squid. Between its sharp beak, suckers, and hooks, the colossal squid has all it needs to grab, hold, and eat large prey.

Safety Features

The squid has many predators to be concerned about, and so it needs to rely on its traits of speed, quickness, and flexibility, along with its complex system of camouflage, in order to protect itself. When in danger, the squid will release a cloud of dark ink, called *sepia*, to momentarily confuse its predator and thereby give itself time to make a quick getaway. The squid also has the ability to blend in with its surrounding environment by changing its skin coloring. Squid have thousands of pigment cells, called *chromatophores*, which expand or contract to change the color or pattern of the squid's skin in order to match their backgrounds, making them practically invisible.

Did You Know?

The only known predator of the colossal squid is the sperm whale. Many times, body parts of the colossal squid have been found inside the stomach linings of these whales.

The colossal squid breaks several records in the natural world. First and foremost, it is the largest invertebrate creature, and the largest creature of prey. It also boasts the largest eyes among all animals; each eye's diameter measures up to twelve inches!

The biggest rival of the colossal squid is the sperm whale. Among the various testimonies of the combats between squid and whales, we read of an incident that occurred approximately forty years ago. Russian whale hunters witnessed a battle between a sperm whale and a colossal squid which ended with the gruesome death of both of them.

A war between a colossal squid and a whale is scary indeed, and the results are brutally harsh. But one cannot overlook the fact that this battle does not begin by choice, but rather by instinct, the instinct that Hashem placed within animals to defend themselves, or, alternatively, to attack a potential victim in order to live, simply put. Every battle of this sort — between a predatory animal and its prey — results from the creature's natural drive toward self-preservation or its desire to win food; it certainly does not involve any personal spite or animosity.

How distressing it is that the human being, the crown jewel of Creation, is often engaged in fights and battles that he chooses willingly and unnecessarily. So much pain, anguish, and loss are caused as a result of fights such as these, battles and conflicts that could have been avoided. Yes, we are born with a drive to be victorious in battle, but as Jews, we know how we can channel that drive properly — to fight among the pages of the Gemara; to wrestle with difficult questions and thorny issues; to battle one's study partner by citing proofs from other Torah sources. This is the type of battle that brings positive and constructive results, and this kind of fight is accepted lovingly by Hashem.

Record Breaker:

In February 2007, a New Zealand fishing vessel caught a colossal squid off the coast of Antarctica. The colossal squid weighed 1,090 pounds and measured around thirty-three feet. This specimen represents the heaviest squid to ever be scientifically documented.

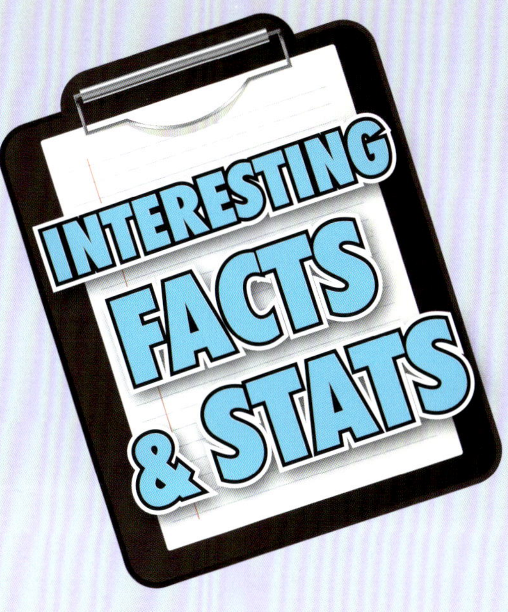

Every squid has three hearts and blue blood.

The sepiolid is the smallest of the squid species. It is less than one inch long and weighs less than a quarter of an ounce.

The Humboldt squid is one of the more aggressive species of the squid. It possesses bioluminescent organs that enable it to glow in the dark. While hunting, it exhibits red and white colors, earning it the nickname Diablo Rojo (Spanish for "Red Devil"). It is a very ferocious predator and is known to even attack sharks. It can grow up to fifteen feet in length and can weigh as much as 100 pounds.

The firefly squid gets its name from the hundreds of bioluminescent photophores (light-producing organs) that cover its body. The glowing light that it emits serves as a warning to predators to keep away. It is also believed that the firefly squid uses its light to communicate with other squid.

Giant squid leave sucker marks on the mouths of whales as they try to avoid being swallowed by them.

The giant-sized eyes of the colossal squid allow it to see objects in the deep, dark depths of the sea.

Some species of squid can swim up to 25 mph.

Squid Trivia

1. The squid and the octopus have some things in common. Which of the following is NOT one of their commonalities?
a. They both have three hearts. **b.** They both are cephalopods.
c. They both have eight limbs. **d.** They both are invertebrates.

2. How many tentacles does a squid have?
a. two **b.** eight **c.** ten **d.** twelve

3. The largest species of the squid is the…
a. giant squid **b.** jumbo squid **c.** Humboldt squid **d.** colossal squid

4. How does the squid protect itself from predators?
a. by camouflage **b.** with its beak **c.** with its tentacles **d.** with its arms

5. Sepia is the name of…
a. the fastest squid species **b.** the ink that the squid releases **c.** the smallest squid **d.** the squid's beak

ANSWERS:
1. c 2. a 3. d 4. a 5. b

Animal Quackers:

Q. Why did the squid leave the U.S. Navy?

A. Because it thought it was better suited to serve in the Arm-y.

TURTLES צב מים

Turtles

There are over 300 different species of turtles worldwide, and they are all reptiles. The turtle spends most of its life in the water and usually has webbed feet for swimming. Of course, whenever one thinks about a turtle, the first thing that usually comes to mind is its shell. The turtle's tough, horny shell is both its home and its coat of armor. The shell covers the turtle's short, broad body from both above and below. Actually, the turtle's shell makes up much of the turtle's skeleton. While most advanced creatures have their skeletons inside their bodies, the turtle wears its skeleton on the outside.

The top part of the shell, called the *carapace*, is really the turtle's backbone and ribs, joined into a solid mass by many bony plates. The carapace is covered by a layer of horny scales. The bottom shell, called the *plastron*, is built around the turtle's breastbone. The carapace and plastron are joined so that there are openings for the turtle's head, four legs, and short tail. There are land turtles and water turtles. Land turtles are slow and clumsy. They would be easy prey for their enemies if not for the protection of their shell, as unlike water turtles, they do not have the option of swimming away from predators. When faced with danger, the land turtle draws its head and legs inside its shell, then pulls the plastron up against the carapace and shuts its home tight. By staying right at home, it is safe from almost all natural enemies.

Painted Turtles

The painted turtle is the most widely distributed turtle in North America. It lives in freshwater habitats such as ponds, lakes, and streams. It is aptly named for its brightly colored markings along its head, neck, and shell. Its face has yellow stripes, with a large, yellow spot and streak behind each eye. The upper shell has red and yellow markings on a black or greenish-brown background.

Although it spends most of its time in the water, the painted turtle often suns itself while lying on a log or rock near a body of water. The painted turtle sleeps underwater, buried in the sand or mud at the bottom of its habitat.

There are various subspecies of the painted turtle, and they vary in size and color. Their sizes usually range from four to ten inches in length.

Young painted turtles face many predators, such as raccoons, skunks, foxes, birds, snakes, and fish. The adults, however, are rarely taken by predators.

Painted turtles live twenty to forty years.

Fast Fact:

During very cold weather, painted turtles hibernate, burying themselves for months in the muddy bottoms of streams and ponds.

I See You!

Unlike land turtles and some freshwater turtles, sea turtles cannot retreat into their shells.

Wacky Fact:

Incredibly, when female sea turtles are ready to lay their eggs, they return to the same beach where they were born, even though it might be thirty years later and the appearance of the beach may have changed!

Sea Turtles

Sea turtles are air-breathing reptiles that are well suited to life in the sea. Their streamlined, hydrodynamic shape; large size; and powerful, paddle-like flippers allow them to dive to great depths and swim long distances. Their flippers are great for propelling them through the water; however, they make it difficult for the turtle to walk on land.

Although sea turtles spend almost all their time in the sea, they always return to the same beach to breed, often traveling huge distances — hundreds, or even thousands, of miles — to get there. Amazingly, female sea turtles will often emerge from the water *within just a few yards* from wherever they nested the time before. After laying their eggs, the female sea turtles will bury them in their nests under the sand, leaving them to hatch on their own. When the baby sea turtles hatch, it may take them as long as a week to dig their way out of the nest. Once they are out, they walk straight into the ocean and begin their life at sea.

Sea turtles are found in all of the major oceans and smaller seas, with the exception of the Arctic Circle, as it is generally too cold for sea turtles there; they prefer more temperate waters. There are seven species of sea turtles, and unfortunately, they are all listed as endangered species. The seven species of sea turtles are: the green sea turtle, the hawksbill, the flatback, the Kemp's ridley turtle, the loggerhead, the leatherback, and the olive ridley turtle. Sea turtles range in size from about two feet to six feet long, depending on the species. The Kemp's ridley turtle is the smallest sea turtle, weighing in at 85 to 100 pounds, and the leatherback sea turtle is the largest, weighing up to 2,000 pounds!

The diet of the sea turtle depends on the species. Some sea turtles are carnivorous, others are herbivores, and some will eat almost anything. Sea turtles tend to eat sea grasses, shrimp, crabs, fish, and jellyfish, depending on what they can find and catch.

Adult sea turtles have very few predators. As long as they can avoid large sharks and steer clear of human fishing nets, they can live more than eighty years in the wild.

Did You Know?

Although sea turtles can remain submerged for hours at a time while resting or sleeping, they usually come up to the water surface several times each hour to breathe.

Any Minute Now...

It takes about three to four months for snapping turtle eggs to hatch!

Wacky Fact:

In the middle of the alligator snapping turtle's tongue is a long, thin piece of pink flesh. When the turtle opens its mouth, this flesh looks like a worm. As soon as a fish swims up close to take a look at the "worm" — snap! — the turtle has a meal!

Snapping Turtles

Snapping turtles are large freshwater reptiles that spend nearly all of their lives in the water. They can remain submerged underwater for up to three hours at a time. Snapping turtles are often considered to be the top predators in their environment. There are two species of snapping turtles: the common snapping turtle and the alligator snapping turtle. Both are noted for their aggressiveness on land, where they will attack large animals, including humans, if they feel threatened. Snapping turtles are also cannibalistic; a larger snapping turtle will attack and devour a smaller snapping turtle. In water, snapping turtles are less aggressive. They do not hunt, but rather lie in wait and ambush unsuspecting prey.

The snapping turtle's main defense mechanism is its powerful, snapping jaws, which enable the turtle to make short work of both attackers and small prey. Snapping turtles also have monstrous, thick claws on their front and back legs, which they use to tear apart food and to climb hills, where they lay their eggs each year. Snapping turtles typically live thirty to fifty years in captivity.

Alligator snapping turtles and common snapping turtles have very different-looking appearances. The alligator snapping turtle has a long head and an almost spiky shell, while the common snapping turtle has a more rounded head and a smoother shell. They are also easily distinguished by size, as the common snapping turtle is smaller than the alligator snapping turtle.

The Common Snapping Turtle

The common snapping turtle inhabits lakes and streams from South America to Canada. It has a large head, powerful jaws, and a long, jagged tail. It can weigh up to sixty pounds, and its shell can grow up to nineteen inches long. It is more aggressive than the alligator snapping turtle, and it will eat just about anything. Its diet includes snails, mussels, fish, and water plants. After catching its prey, the common snapping turtle uses its hooked jaws to tear the food into tiny pieces.

The Alligator Snapping Turtle

The alligator snapping turtle is generally found in the more southern waters of the United States. It has hooked jaws, prickly scales on its neck, and a long, alligator-like tail. It is the largest freshwater turtle in North America, reaching lengths of two and a half feet and weighing up to 200 pounds. Its diet consists mainly of fish.

Fast Fact:

Snapping turtles like to bury themselves in mud, with only their nostrils and eyes exposed. This tactic is used as a means of ambushing their prey.

Selling Like Hot Cakes

In the sixties and seventies, Mary River turtles were very popular pets in Australia. Every year 15,000 were sold to pet shops for a decade!

Did You Know?

The yellow-spotted river turtle is an example of a side-necked turtle. Side-necked turtles do not pull their heads directly into their shells; instead, they bend their neck sideways to tuck their heads under the rim of their shells.

River Turtles

River turtles can be found inhabiting freshwater environments all around the world, from slow-moving rivers and streams to the nearly still waters of ponds and lakes. There are numerous different species of river turtles, and many of them are listed as endangered species today.

As with other turtle species, river turtles are fairly solitary animals, but females can be seen gathering together in large groups on river banks to lay their eggs. Depending on the species, river turtles can lay 5 to 100 soft, leathery eggs, which are then buried in the sand by the mother turtles. After a couple of months, the baby river turtles hatch and head straight for the water.

Due to the relatively large size of the river turtle and the fact that it has a hard, protective shell, there are few animals that prey upon the adults. People are the main predators of both the river turtle and its eggs, which are eaten as a royal delicacy in many of the river turtle's native regions. Also, animals such as foxes, dogs, snakes, and birds eat the eggs of the river turtle that are buried in the sand.

Most species of river turtles have an omnivorous diet that is primarily made up of aquatic plants, grasses, and leaves. Many river turtle species also prey on fish and mollusks in the water, along with small reptiles and amphibians.

The Mary River turtle is the most commonly known species of river turtles, as they are the most popular freshwater turtles to keep as pets. The Mary River turtle is native to the Mary River in Queensland, Australia. Like a few other freshwater turtles, the Mary River turtle can extract oxygen from the water with the gill-like structures it has in its tail; therefore, it can spend more time underwater without needing to surface.

The yellow-spotted river turtle is one of the largest species of river turtles found in South America, as it can grow up to eighteen inches long. It inhabits the large lakes and tributaries of the Amazon Basin, and is easily identified by its yellow spots on the side of its head (hence its name).

Fast Fact:

A unique feature of the male Mary River turtle is its tail, which can measure over two-thirds of the length of its shell.

Wet, Wild, &

Turtle or Tortoise?

One of the major differences between a turtle and a tortoise is that the turtle lives in water, while the tortoise lives on land. But there are other differences as well:

- **Shell:** The shell of a turtle is flat, lightweight, and streamlined — characteristics that aid in swimming, while the shell of a tortoise is very large, quite heavy, and dome-shaped, to provide protection from predators.
- **Body Type:** Unlike the turtle, the tortoise does not have webbed feet; its feet are round and stumpy, which is better for walking on land. Tortoises that live in hot, dry environments use their powerful forelimbs to dig burrows. When it's too hot in the sun, they dip underground to cool off.
- **Lifespan**: Tortoises generally have long lifespans. There are documented accounts of tortoises exceeding 150 years of age. There are also undocumented accounts of tortoises living 250 to 300 years of age! On the other hand, the lifespan of a turtle is estimated to be between twenty and fifty years, with the sea turtle in particular having an estimated lifespan of sixty to eighty years.

Shell Station

As mentioned before, the shell of the turtle is made up of two parts: the carapace and the plastron. This is whether the shell is flat or domed. Both the carapace and the plastron are made of bone, including about fifty to sixty rib and back bones in the upper shell and a fusion of clavicle and rib bones in the lower shell. The turtle's shell grows along with the turtle. It never falls off, is never too big, and is never too small. Made from the turtle's rib cage and spine, the turtle's shell is attached to the internal bones of its body.

The shell is covered with *scutes*, which are overlapping pieces of keratin (the fibrous protein also found in bones, nails, and teeth). This gives the shell a protective coating. Scutes grow in layers and build up outward, with the oldest scute layers on the outside. With most turtle species, as the turtle and its shell grow, the outside layers of scutes on the shell peel or shed away and are replaced by new, larger, and healthier scutes. The scutes do not shed all at once, but continuously, in small pieces.

Wacky Fact:

Sea turtles are able to drink salty sea water, because they have glands near their eyes that remove the excess salt.

Wondrous

Miles Logger

Natal homing refers to the migrating process by which some animals are able to return to their birthplace to reproduce. Sea turtles are the most commonly known sea creatures that exhibit natal homing. As mentioned, these migrations often take the sea turtles hundreds and even thousands of miles. One extraordinary example of this is that of the loggerhead sea turtle.

The loggerhead sea turtle travels over 9,000 miles round trip during its migration. This spectacular journey begins as soon as the loggerhead hatchling is able to leave its nest. Each hatchling is on its own as it heads directly toward the ocean to begin its migration around the entire North Atlantic basin. Young loggerheads that survive this epic migration (most do not) will return to the coastal waters of North America in about six to twelve years' time! This journey is among the longest and most incredible migrations in the entire animal kingdom.

It is not known exactly how adult turtles are able to navigate to their birthplace beaches; however, researchers think they may use a number of clues, including ocean currents, the earth's magnetic field, and water chemistry.

One Thousand to One Shot

Only one of one thousand sea turtle hatchlings survive to maturity. Animals like skunks and raccoons often follow land and freshwater turtles to their nests, then sit and wait for the eggs as they are being laid in order to eat them. If they missed the egg-laying, they dig up the eggs afterward and dine on them. Then, when the hatchlings of the remaining eggs emerge and start crawling toward the ocean, they are often consumed by birds and other animals. In the water, they can be attacked by sharks or other big fish.

To make up for the loss of eggs and hatchlings, the Creator has given turtles a long life. Many species of turtles live more than eighty years. A pet turtle could be in a family for generations! During this time span, they can reproduce themselves in sufficient numbers to perpetuate their species.

Did You Know?

Fishermen are likely to make better catches in places where turtles are plentiful. This is because turtles eat jellyfish, the sea creatures that drive many fish away.

One of the most noted characteristics of the turtle is its slow and steady pace. The patience that the turtle exhibits is quite remarkable. For example, it takes a mother turtle at least thirty minutes to crawl up the beach from the sea, two hours to create a nest, an hour to lay 50 to 100 eggs, and another half an hour to crawl back to the water.

The slow and steady approach of the turtle should teach us the value of composure. The mishnah in *Pirkei Avos* (6:6) lists the virtue of "*yishuv*" as one of the forty-eight qualities through which Torah is acquired. Literally, "*yishuv*" means dwelling, sitting, or resting. The commentators understand this virtue as either a state of mind — studying with composure and careful diligence — or spending sufficient time learning Torah.

Many people tend to speed through the basic texts of the Torah. They are anxious to go beyond the basics and delve into the Gemara and more advanced Torah study. When one tastes the sweetness of an intricate *sugya*, he understandably becomes very excited and wants to jump ahead for more. He may be anxious to advance his own insights, to formulate his own ideas, to make his own personal acquisition of the Torah, and may not want to be slowed down by the mastering of Torah fundamentals first. There is no denying that the sheer excitement of plumbing the depths of the Torah — and thus making sense out of the whole universe — inspires a soul and stirs it to creativity.

However, our mishnah charges us with an important word of caution. We must take care to study with patience and diligence. In all our enthusiasm to acquire Torah knowledge, it must still always be based on the slow and steady, on the mastering of the fundamental texts as well as the nuances and languages of the Sages. There are no shortcuts.

The trait of the turtle reminds us that although it is usually an advantage to do things in a quick and lively way, it is certainly no good to be carelessly hasty. Very often one can accomplish more by doing things slowly but surely.

Record Breaker:

The Guangzhou Aquarium in China claims that one of their sea turtles is over 400 years old!

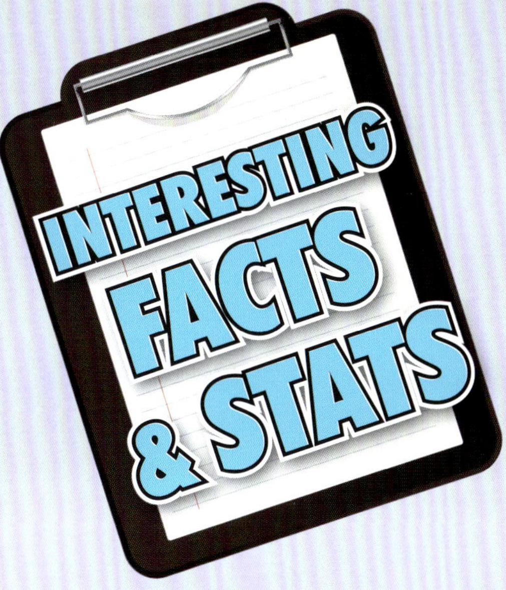

- A group of turtles is called a bale.
- Sea turtles can swim up to 35 mph.
- A box turtle can carry a weight 200 times greater than its own. If a person was that strong, he would be able to carry ten cars on his back!
- The bog turtle is the smallest North American turtle, measuring about four inches in length.
- Turtles don't have teeth, but instead have horny ridges that are serrated and sharp, on their upper and lower jaws. These horny ridges enable the turtles to cut hard substances such as shells.
- Leatherback sea turtles are among the most highly migratory animals on earth, traveling as many as 10,000 miles or more each year between foraging grounds, in search of jellyfish.
- Oil extracted from turtles (especially leatherback sea turtles) possesses medicinal qualities. African natives use the oil to cure asthma and skin rashes.
- The common snapping turtle is not an ideal pet. Its neck is very flexible, and it is able to bite its handler even if picked up by the sides of its shell.
- Turtles have good eyesight and an excellent sense of smell.

Turtle Trivia

1. What is the top part of the turtle's shell called?
a. plastron **b.** capsule **c.** dome **d.** carapace

2. How many species of sea turtles are there?
a. 2 **b.** 7 **c.** over 300 **d.** no one knows for sure

3. All turtles…
a. are reptiles **b.** have shells **c.** are also tortoises **d.** a and b

4. What percentage of baby sea turtles actually make it to adulthood?
a. 1% **b.** 10% **c.** 25% **d.** 50%

5. Which is the largest species of the snapping turtle?
a. Galápagos **b.** common snapping turtle **c.** alligator snapping turtle **d.** giant snapper

ANSWERS:
1. d 2. b 3. d 4. a 5. c

Animal Quackers:

Q. What do turtles use to communicate with each other?

A. Shell-phones!

WHALES לוויתן

Whales

Whales are large, intelligent sea creatures that belong to the group of aquatic mammals called *cetaceans*. The word "cetacean" is used to describe all whales, dolphins, and porpoises in the order *Cetacea*. Whales range in size from less than nine feet long (the length of the dwarf sperm whale) to up to 100 feet long (the length of the giant blue whale, which is the largest creature in the animal kingdom).

Unlike fish that breathe using gills, cetaceans breathe through their blowholes. Blowholes are a whale's nostrils and are located on the top of the whale's head. There are two types of cetaceans: toothed whales and baleen whales. Toothed whales have one blowhole, while baleen whales have two. Toothed whales have peg-like teeth that they use to catch fish, squid, and marine mammals, all of which they swallow whole. Baleen whales have hundreds of comb-like plates of baleen (a flexible yet durable material that is used as a filter) hanging from their upper jaws. Baleen whales feed by gulping large amounts of water containing thousands of fish or plankton, and then forcing the water out in between the baleen plates, which leaves the prey trapped inside. The prey is then swallowed whole.

In this section, we will be exploring two types of baleen whales and two types of toothed whales.

The Beluga Whale

The beluga whale, also called the white whale, is a small, toothed whale that can be thirteen to twenty feet long. It is easily recognized by its white coloring, blunt head, and extremely bulbous melon. (The melon is the fatty organ located at the center of toothed whales' foreheads. It is used for echolocation.) Another distinctive trait of the beluga whale is that it does not have a dorsal fin, which allows it to move easily under floating ice.

Belugas are very social animals and travel together in groups, called *pods*, of two to twenty-five whales, with an average pod size of ten whales. A pod will hunt and migrate as a group. Belugas live in frigid Arctic and sub-Arctic waters, but some groups migrate south to warmer waters in the summer. During migrations, several pods may join together, forming groups of 200 to 10,000 belugas!

Belugas feed on fish, squid, octopus, crustaceans, and worms. The beluga's main predators are polar bears and killer whales. Beluga whales' white coloring protects them by allowing them to camouflage themselves in the polar ice caps in the Arctic, although young belugas are not white; at birth, belugas are bluish gray, dark gray, or brown. Their color eventually fades to white by six years of age.

The average lifespan of a beluga whale is thirty-five to fifty years in the wild.

Fast Fact:

Unlike most other whales, the beluga has a flexible neck (the seven vertebrae in its neck are not fused together). This allows the whale to turn its head in all directions — up and down and side to side.

A Heavy Heart

The heart of the average humpback whale weighs about 430 pounds!

Wacky Fact:

Adult humpback whales fast for a few months at a time during the summer while migrating to warm waters. They live off of their fat reserves, while their young feed on milk from their mothers.

The Humpback Whale

The humpback whale is a species of the baleen whale and is known for its majestic "songs." It is the noisiest of all whales — its "songs" can last twenty minutes and can be repeated for hours on end. They have a variety of complex sounds that include frequencies beyond the threshold of human hearing, and their "songs" can be heard from great distances throughout the oceans.

The humpback whale is one of the larger species of whales. It can reach up to fifty-two feet in length, and it can weigh over 80,000 pounds. It has extremely long flippers that are up to one-third of its body length; these are the largest flippers of any whale! The humpback whale has a distinctive hump of fatty tissue just in front of its dorsal fin (the fin on its back). It also has a bulky head with bumpy tubercles (knobs), and its skin is usually scarred and has patches covered with barnacles. The humpback is a powerful swimmer and is quite the acrobat. It uses its massive tail fin, called a *fluke*, to propel itself through the ocean, and it regularly leaps and twirls completely out of the water, high above the surface, slapping at the water with its flippers and flukes.

Like all baleen whales, the humpback whale has two blowholes and does not have teeth. It primarily feeds off of krill and plankton. Humpbacks are gulpers, filter feeders that alternatively swim and then gulp a mouthful of plankton or fish. The humpback will eat 4,500 to 6,000 pounds of food each day during the feeding season.

Humpbacks are found in all oceans around the world. They spend the summer months in the colder polar waters, and then, in the winter, they migrate south to the warmer tropical waters. There are three separate populations of humpback whales: one in the North Pacific, a second in the North Atlantic, and a third in the southern hemisphere. None of the three whale populations interact with each other.

The average humpback whale will travel up to 16,000 miles a year during its migration. Female humpback whales tend to give birth to their young during the winter months, when they are in the warmer, southern waters.

Humpback whales have a life expectancy of forty-five to fifty years.

Did You Know?

The humpback whale was given its name because of the shape of its dorsal (back) fin and because of the motion the whale makes when it arches its back out of the water in preparation for a dive.

Family Unity

Many killer whales live with their mothers for their entire lives!

Wacky Fact:

The killer whale is very creative when it comes to capturing prey. One tactic it uses is to vomit up partially eaten fish in order to lure seabirds, which it then gobbles up.

The Killer Whale

The killer whale, also referred to as the orca whale or orca, is an aquatic mammal that inhabits all the world's oceans, both hot and cold, from the freezing waters of the North and South Poles to the tropical seas. Killer whales are toothed whales that belong to the order *Delphinidae*, which means that the killer whale is actually a dolphin. In fact, the killer whale is the largest member of the dolphin family. There are about five different species of killer whales in the oceans.

The killer whale has a long, rounded body with a large dorsal fin (over six feet high) in the middle of its back. The killer whale's black-and-white body is its most identifiable feature. The male killer whales are larger than the females, generally growing to be twenty to thirty feet long and weighing up to ten tons. The females typically grow to be sixteen to twenty-three feet long and weigh up to six tons.

The killer whale is one of the fastest marine mammals and can swim as fast as 30 mph. Also, it is common for a killer whale to swim more than fifty miles without stopping.

Killer whales are highly social and group themselves in matrilineal family groups. They hunt in pods that normally contain six to forty killer whales, although some pods may combine to form a group of 100 or more. Killer whales are often referred to as "the wolves of the sea," as they are dominant predators and hunt in packs in a similar way to wolves on land. All pods use effective, cooperative hunting techniques that can be likened to the behavior of wolf packs. On a typical day, an average killer whale will eat over 450 pounds of food, which usually includes over twenty different species of marine mammals and more than thirty different species of large fish. A killer whale's prey is generally made up of large fish, seals, sea lions, sea birds, and marine mammals.

Like their dolphin cousins, killer whales are extremely vocal creatures. They communicate with each other using clicks and whistles in a process known as *echolocation*. Killer whales are known to be quite noisy when hunting and much calmer and quieter when they are resting.

Female killer whales give birth to one baby killer whale roughly once every five years, after a seventeen-month pregnancy. At birth, killer whale babies, called *calves*, weigh about 400 pounds and are about eight feet long.

In the wild, female killer whales can live fifty to ninety years, while male killer whales usually live thirty to sixty years.

Fast Fact:

Killer whales have forty to fifty teeth that are up to four inches long.

Maximum Minkes!
Minke whales are the most abundant species of baleen whales. It is estimated that there are almost 800,000 minke whales worldwide.

Did You Know?

The name "minke" comes from a Norwegian whaler named Meincke, who incorrectly identified these small baleen whales as their larger cousins, the blue whales.

The Minke Whale

The minke whale (pronounced ming-kee) is a relatively small baleen whale with an average length of twenty-four to thirty feet. Like other baleen whales, the females are just a bit larger (one to two feet) than the males when fully grown. There are two recognized species of minke whales: the common minke whale (also called the northern minke whale) and the Antarctic minke whale (also called the southern minke whale). There is a debate whether or not the dwarf minke whale should be classified as a possible third species.

Minke whales can be found swimming throughout the world's oceans, from tropical climates to the upper and lower polar hemispheres, though they tend to prefer living in colder climates than tropical ones. These whales are most commonly found swimming in the northern Atlantic and southern Antarctic oceans. Minke whales are mostly solitary mammals, and many tend to live alone. Some travel in small pods consisting of only two to three whales.

The minke whale's stocky body has a thick layer of blubber. The upper part of its body is a black or dark gray color, and its underside is white. It has two blowholes, two long flippers (which make up to one-eighth of its body size), a small dorsal fin, and ridges along its back, close to its tail. The minke whale is nicknamed the "sharp-headed finner" and the "little piked whale" because of its triangular, pointed, and narrow snout. This snout is the first thing that is visible when the minke whale leaps out of the water.

The minke whale is a very good swimmer and normally swims 3 to 16 mph; however, if it is in danger, it is able to swim as fast as 24 mph. The minke whale is also known for its deep dives. Before making a deep dive, it jumps in the air, arches its back, and may twist around in the atmosphere before reentering the water. It is able to stay underwater for up to twenty-five minutes before surfacing for air, although it usually comes up for air every ten to twelve minutes.

The minke whale's gestation period is about ten months long, and it usually gives birth to one calf near the surface of shallow waters. When it is born, the calf is about nine feet long and weighs about 1,000 pounds. Within ten seconds of its birth, the newborn instinctively swims to the surface for its first breath of air. The mother whale helps the calf reach the surface with her flippers. Within thirty minutes of its birth, the baby whale is able to swim.

Fast Fact:

The minke whale is the second smallest baleen whale. The only baleen whale that is smaller than the minke is the pygmy right whale.

Wet, Wild, &

Deadly Hunters

Killer whales hunt in deadly pods of up to forty whales. Their creativity and intelligence are quite evident as they perform a variety of complex hunting tactics when hunting for prey. In extremely cold climates, killer whales hit floating chunks of ice where seals are resting, in an attempt to knock them into the sea. Killer whales also try to make waves to force their prey off the ice. Another sly hunting tactic that is used is when a killer whale leaps out of the water and temporarily beaches itself on the ice, just to coax seals into the water. When the frightened seals jump into the water, the members of the pod of whales, lying in wait, gobble them up.

Yet another technique that is used is known as *carousel fishing*. A small group of killer whales surrounds a school of fish such as salmon and either releases bursts of bubbles or flashes their white undersides in order to round the fish up. The fish are then contained in a tight, defensive ball close to the surface of the sea. The killer whales then slap the "ball" with their tails, stunning or killing the fish instantly.

Bubble Trouble

One method that the humpback whales use to hunt their prey is blowing bubbles.

This method of hunting is known as *bubble net feeding*. Bubble net feeding involves anywhere from four to twenty humpback whales, all working together to herd schools of fish such as herring.

The way the bubble net trap works is as follows: A group of humpbacks will dive down to herring schools, where one whale (the bubble-blower) will descend below the school of herring and swim around and around it, releasing a ring of bubbles from its blowhole. As this air rises to the surface, it forms a curtain of bubbles that acts as a physical barrier to frighten the herring and keep the school of them in place. While this is happening, another whale in the group will sing resonating vocalizations, which frighten the fish even more and cause them to swim together in tight balls within the bubble net. The whales then position themselves below the tight balls of fish and lunge, mouths open, to the surface, through the center of the bubble net. This motion drives the fish to the surface, where they are trapped from all sides — the surface of the water above, the bubble curtain on the sides, and the open mouths of the whales below.

Wacky Fact:

Humpback whales sing their "songs" while hanging vertically, head down, in the water. It is also interesting to note that only male humpback whales have been recorded singing.

Wondrous

Species of Last Choice

The minke whale was among the last species of baleen whales to be hunted by whalers. It is believed that their smaller size made them less desirable by whalers, as they could find more value with the larger-sized whale species. However, during the late twentieth century, the number of minke whales killed by whalers rose sharply.

As the larger whales became scarce (and gained protected status), minke whales became a popular target of whalers. From the 1920s, the killing of minkes by whalers increased steadily along the coast of Norway. When whale populations decreased drastically in the late 1940s, the International Whaling Commission was established to manage them. The Commission decided on the number of whales that were permitted to be killed. However, whale populations still continued to decline.

In the early 1980s, the minke whale became the most heavily hunted baleen whale. In 1985/1986, a worldwide suspension on whaling was put in place, banning all whaling. However, in 1994, after intense pressure from Japan, Norway, and Denmark, the International Whaling Commission gave permission for the minke whale to be hunted for scientific purposes. Today, the minke whale is still being hunted in these countries as a source of food and for scientific research.

Canaries of the Sea

Beluga whales are very vocal communicators. Belugas are also called "sea canaries," because their songs and chatter sometimes sound like bird songs. They have an incredible, diversified language which includes clicks, squeals, cackles, and whistles. Besides using their vocalization to communicate with each other, belugas also use it to locate food and to navigate the ocean.

How does vocalization help belugas in these ways? Belugas use echolocation to locate their prey, and to travel safely in the deep, dark waters. They produce a series of clicks that pass through their melon, which acts as an acoustic lens to focus the sounds into a beam that is propelled through the water. These sounds travel through the water at a very fast speed (four times faster than the speed of sound in the air). The sound waves bounce off objects in the water and return as echoes that are heard and interpreted by the whale. This helps the whale determine the distance, speed, size, and shape of the objects within the beam of sound.

Did You Know?

The beluga whale can mimic a variety of sounds — including human speech!

Every Yom Kippur we read the *haftorah* that relates the story of Yonah and the whale. Hashem sent Yonah as a messenger to the city of Ninveh. The people in Ninveh had sinned to such a degree that Hashem was ready to destroy the city — unless the people there did *teshuvah* immediately. Yonah was to relay this message to them — but he did not want to fulfill this mission.

Yonah was concerned for the welfare of the Jewish people, who were also guilty of grievous sins. He feared that the evil people of Ninveh would heed his warning and repent, which would make the Jewish people look bad and bring Hashem's anger on them. Therefore, Yonah chose to flee from his mission, rather than bring down retribution on the heads of his people.

Yonah escaped on a ship, but a sudden storm threatened to tear the ship apart. The sailors cast lots, and Yonah was tossed into the sea, where he was swallowed by a whale. From the belly of the whale, Yonah cried out to Hashem and pleaded for deliverance. Hashem answered Yonah's prayer, and the whale spit him out onto the shore. Yonah then immediately went to Ninveh and relayed Hashem's message to the people. The people repented, and the city of Ninveh was spared.

There are many lessons to be learned from this story. We learn about the power of *teshuvah* — how it can save an entire city from destruction. But we can also learn a deeper lesson, about a person's obligation to obey Hashem's command, no matter how he feels about doing it.

Yonah certainly had no illusions about thwarting the Divine plan; he simply had such an overpowering love for the Jewish people that he could not bear to be the agent of their misfortune. But Hashem did not choose to send a different agent to Ninveh. Instead, He sent a storm and a whale to force Yonah to accept his mission. The message to Yonah was clear: he had no right to weigh the pros and cons of obeying Hashem's command. A person has to subjugate himself completely to the Divine will, to obey without question, reservation, or rationalization.

In our own lives, we sometimes bend the rules to suit our convenience. We fall into the trap of seeking a middle ground to satisfy our desires. We rationalize and we compromise and we seek to escape the strictures imposed on us by our innermost conscience. But in actuality, as Yonah discovered so painfully, it is not for us to make judgments about the Divine will. Although it is sometimes difficult, we must always accept Hashem's will wholeheartedly and completely.

Record Breaker:

The world record for the longest mammal ever recorded belongs to a female blue whale measuring 110 feet 2 inches. This whale was found in 1909 at Grytviken, South Georgia, in the South Atlantic.

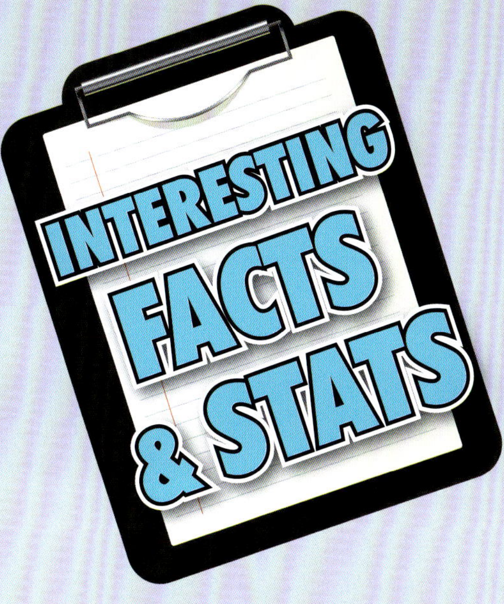

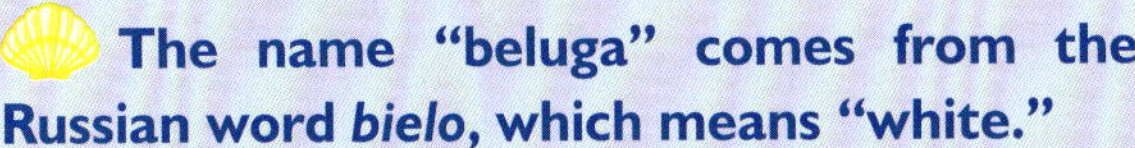

- The name "beluga" comes from the Russian word *bielo*, which means "white."
- Cetaceans are the only mammals, other than the manatee, that live their entire lives in the ocean.
- The name "Cetacean" comes from the Latin word *cetus*, meaning "a large sea animal," and the Greek word *ketos*, meaning "sea monster."
- Whales have excellent hearing. They do not have external ears, but have tiny ear openings behind each eye. They can also tell the direction of sound underwater.
- Whales have hair all over their body, but the hair is very thin, so it is difficult to notice.
- Since whales cannot breathe underwater, they need to be awake just about all the time in order to be able to come up to the surface to breathe. So, whales "sleep" by resting one half of their brain at a time. While one half of the brain sleeps, the other half of the brain stays awake to make sure the whale breathes and to be on the alert for any danger.
- Like all mammals, whales are warm-blooded, produce milk to feed their young, and have body hair.
- The sperm whale has the largest brain in the world. It can weigh up to twenty pounds!
- Whales can't breathe through their mouths, because their mouths are connected directly to their stomachs.

Whale Trivia

1. A killer whale is a…
a. baleen whale **b.** large fish **c.** member of the dolphin family **d.** a and c

2. All toothed whales have…
a. a dorsal fin and one blowhole **b.** teeth and two blowholes
c. a dorsal fin and teeth **d.** teeth and one blowhole

3. Whales breathe through their…
a. blowhole and mouth **b.** blowhole only **c.** mouth only **d.** eyes

4. Which statement is false? The beluga whale…
a. is white throughout its life **b.** is also called the white whale
c. is a toothed whale **d.** is a mammal

5. Which species of the whale has the largest flippers?
a. blue whale **b.** humpback whale **c.** sperm whale **d.** killer whale

ANSWERS:
1. c 2. d 3. b 4. a 5. b

Animal Quackers:

Q. What do whales like to chew?

A. Blubber gum.

Photo Credits

Axolotl
Page 6: iStockphoto/ Thinkstock
Page 7: Lukas Blazek/ Dreamstime
Page 8: Sombra/ Bigstock, Dreamstime, Bigstock
Page 9: Raman Zaremba/ Dreamstime, Design Pics/ Thinkstock, Lajos Endredl/ Dreamstime
Page 10: iStockphoto/ Thinkstock
Page 11: Miroslava Kopecka/ Dreamstime, Lukas Blazek/ Dreamstime

Coral
Page 12: Digital Vision / Getty Images/ Thinkstock
Page 13: Getty Images/ iStockphoto/ Thinkstock
Page 14: Getty Images/ iStockphoto/ Thinkstock
Page 15: Getty Images/ Photo Disc Green/ Thinkstock, Getty Images/ Hemera/ Thinkstock, Getty Images/ iStockphoto/ Thinkstock, Getty Images/ iStockphoto, Thinkstock
Page 16: Getty Images/ iStockphoto/ Thinkstock
Page 17: Getty Images/ iStockphoto/ Thinkstock, Getty Images/ iStockphoto/ Thinkstock

Crocodile
Page 18: Getty Images/ Hemera/ Thinkstock
Page 19: Getty Images/ iStockphoto/ Thinkstock
Page 20: Getty Images/ iStockphoto/ Thinkstock, Anup Shah/ Photo Disc/ Getty Images/ Thinkstock/ George Doyle and Claran Griffin/ Stockbyte/ Getty Images/ Thinkstock
Page 21: Getty Images/ iStockphoto/ Thinkstock, Jupiter Images/ Photos.com/ Getty Images/ Thinkstock, Getty Images/ iStockphoto/ Thinkstock
Page 22: Surz/ Bigstock
Page 23: Getty Images/ iStockphoto/ Thinkstock, Getty Images/ Hemera/ Thinkstock

Dolphin
Page 24: Getty Images/ iStockphoto/ Thinkstock
Page 25: Getty Images/ iStockphoto/ Thinkstock
Page 26: Getty Images/ iStockphoto/ Thinkstock, Getty Images/ iStockphoto/ Thinkstock, Abiestock.com/ Getty Images/ Thinkstock
Page 27: Fuse/ Getty Images/ Thinkstock, Getty Images/ iStockphoto, Thinkstock
Page 28: Tim Brakefield/ Stockbyte/ Getty Images/ Thinkstock
Page 29: Getty Images/ iStockphoto/ Thinkstock, Fuse/ Getty Images/ Thinkstock

Duck
Page 30: Getty Images/ iStockphoto/ Thinkstock
Page 31: Digital Vision/ Thinkstock
Page 32: Getty Images/ iStockphoto/ Thinkstock, Getty Images/ istockphoto/ Thinkstock, Getty Images/ istockphoto/ Thinkstock, Getty Images/ iStockphoto/ Thinkstock
Page 33: Getty Images/ istockphoto/ Thinkstock, Getty Images/ istockphoto/ Thinkstock, Getty Images/ istockphoto/ Thinkstock
Page 34: Getty Images/ iStockphoto/ Thinkstock
Page 35: Getty Images/ iStockphoto/ Thinkstock, Image Source/ Getty Images/ Thinkstock

Eel
Page 36: Getty Images/ iStockphoto/ Thinkstock
Page 37: Getty Images/ iStockphoto/ Thinkstock
Page 38: Getty Images/ iStockphoto/ Thinkstock, Getty Images/ iStockphoto/ Thinkstock
Page 39: Hemera/ Getty Images/ Thinkstock, Youthstock/ Dreamstime
Page 40: Hemera/ Getty Images/ Thinkstock
Page 41: Getty Images/ iStockphoto/ Thinkstock, Getty Images/ iStockphoto/ Thinkstock

Elephant Seal
Page 42: Getty Images/ iStockphoto/ Thinkstock
Page 43: Fuse/ Getty Images/ Thinkstock
Page 44: Getty Images/ iStockphoto/ Thinkstock, Hotshots Worldwide/ Bigstock, Getty Images/ iStockphoto/ Thinkstock
Page 45: Fuse/ Getty Images/ Thinkstock, Jupiter Images/ Photos.com/ Getty Images/ Thinkstock, Red Jeniks/ Dreamstime
Page 46: Hemera/ Getty Images/ Thinkstock
Page 47: Getty Images/ iStockphoto/ Thinkstock, Tom Bakerfield/ Stockbyte/ Getty Images/ Thinkstock

Frogs
Page 48: Kikker Dirk/ Bigstock, Getty Images/ iStockphoto/ Thinkstock, Getty Images/ iStockphoto/ Thinkstock, Getty Images/ iStockphoto/ Thinkstock
Page 49: Jupiter Images/ Photos.com/ Getty Images/ Thinkstock
Page 50: Getty Images/ iStockphoto/ Thinkstock
Page 51: Getty Images/ iStockphoto/ Thinkstock
Page 52: Fuse/ Getty Images/ Thinkstock
Page 53: Getty Images/ iStockphoto/ Thinkstock
Page 54: Getty Images/ iStockphoto/ Thinkstock
Page 55: Getty Images/ iStockphoto/ Thinkstock
Page 56: Purestock/ Getty Images/ Thinkstock, Getty Images/ iStockphto/ Thinkstock, Ingraham Publishing/ Getty Images/ Thinkstock
Page 57: Getty Images/ iStockphoto/ Thinkstock, John Foxx/ Stockbyte/ Getty Images/ Thinkstock, Hemera Technologies, Photo Objects
Page 58: Getty Images/ iStockphoto/ Thinkstock
Page 59: Getty Images/ iStockphoto/ Thinkstock, Getty Images/ iStockphoto/ Thinkstock

Jellyfish
Page 60: Purestock/ Getty Images/ Thinkstock
Page 61: Getty Images/ iStockphoto/ Thinkstock
Page 62: Zonar, Getty Images, Zepherwind/ Dreamstime, Getty Images/ iStockphoto/ Thinkstock
Page 63: Lienkie/ Dreamstime/ Dawn Burns/ Bigstock
Page 64: Getty Images/ iStockphoto/ Thinkstock
Page 65: Hemera/ Getty Images/ iStockphoto/ Thinkstock,Fuse/ Getty Images/ iStockphoto/ Thinkstock

Manta Ray
Page 66: Getty Images/ iStockphoto/ Thinkstock
Page 67: Kjurgan/ Dreamstime
Page 68: Hbuchholz/ Dreamstime/ Getty Images/ iStockphoto/ Thinkstock
Page 69: Getty Images/ iStockphoto/ Thinkstock, Subsurface, Dreamstime
Page 70: iStockphoto/ Thinkstock
Page 71: Images/ Thinkstock, iStockphoto/ Thinkstock

Octopus
Page 72: iStockphoto/ Thinkstock
Page 73: iStockphoto/ Thinkstock
Page 74: Hemera, iStockphoto, iStockphoto
Page 75: iStockphoto, iStockphoto, Hemera
Page 76: Planctan video/ Bigstock
Page 77: iStockphoto, Hemera

Penguin
Page 78: Fuse, Konstantin Kalishko/ Bistock/ Jan Martin Will/ Big-

stock/ Jupiter Images/ Photos.com
Page 79: iStockphoto, iStockphoto, Dabio Hidalgo/ Bigstock
Page 82: Fuse
Page 83: Jupiter Images/ Photos.com
Page 84: iStockphoto
Page 85: Fuse
Page 86: iStockphoto, Fuse/ Getty Images, iStockphoto
Page 87: Getty Images/ iStockphoto/ Thinkstock, Getty Images/ iStockphoto/ Thinkstock
Page 88: Fuse, Getty Images
Page 89: Vladamir Selverstov/ Bigstock, Getty Images/ iStock-photo/ Thinkstock

Pirana

Page 90: Jupiter Images/ Photos.com/ Getty Images
Page 91: Getty Images/ iStockphoto/ Thinkstock
Page 92: Bigstock, Hemera/ Getty Images, Igor Koralchuk/ Bigstock
Page 93: Photos.com/ Getty Images
Page 94: / Bigstock
Page 95: Getty Images/ iStockphoto/ Thinkstock, Getty Images/ iStockphoto/ Thinkstock

Seahorse

Page 96: Getty Images/ iStockphoto/ Thinkstock
Page 97: Getty Images/ iStockphoto/ Thinkstock
Page 98: Getty Images/ iStockphoto/ Thinkstock, Getty Images/ iStockphoto/ Thinkstock, Getty Images/ iStockphoto/ Thinkstock
Page 99: Getty Images/ iStockphoto/ Thinkstock, Linda Bucklin, Getty Images/ iStockphoto/ Thinkstock
Page 100: Getty Images/ iStockphoto/ Thinkstock
Page 101: Getty Images/ iStockphoto/ Thinkstock, Medioimages/ Photodisc/ Getty Images

Sea Otter

Page 102: Abbott/ Bigstock
Page 103: Fuse
Page 104: Getty Images/ iStockphoto/ Thinkstock, Jupiter Images/ photos.com/ Getty Images/ Bigstock
Page 105: Getty Images/ iStockphoto/ Thinkstock, Getty Images/ iStockphoto/ Thinkstock, Getty Images/ iStockphoto/ Thinkstock,
Page 106: Getty Images/ iStockphoto/ Thinkstock
Page 107: Getty Images/ iStockphoto/ Thinkstock, Getty Images/ iStockphoto/ Thinkstock

Sharks

Page 108: Getty Images/ iStockphoto/ Thinkstock, Bigstock, Getty Images/ iStockphoto/ Thinkstock, Getty Images, Design Pics RF/ Thinkstock
Page 109: Getty Images/ iStockphoto/ Thinkstock
Page 110: Getty Images, Fuse, Thinkstock
Page 111: Getty Images/ iStockphoto/ Thinkstock
Page 112: Getty Images/ iStockphoto/ Thinkstock
Page 113: Getty Images/ iStockphoto/ Thinkstock
Page 114: Getty Images/ iStockphoto/ Thinkstock
Page 115: Getty Images/ iStockphoto/ Thinkstock
Page 116: Getty Images/ Fuse/ Thinkstock, Getty Images/ Image Source/ Thinkstock
Page 117: Getty Images/ iStockphoto/ Thinkstock, Getty Images/ iStockphoto/ Thinkstock
Page 118: Getty Images/ iStockphoto/ Thinkstock
Page 119: Getty Images/ iStockphoto/ Thinkstock, Getty Images/ iStockphoto/ Thinkstock

Snail

Page 120: Getty Images/ iStockphoto/ Thinkstock
Page 121: Stockbyte/ Thinkstock
Page 122: Getty Images/ iStockphoto/ Thinkstock, Getty Images/ iStockphoto/ Thinkstock, Getty Images/ Ingraham Publishing/ Thinkstock
Page 123: Getty Images/ iStockphoto/ Thinkstock, DJ712/ Dreamstime
Page 124: David Acosta Alleyly/ Bigstock
Page 125: Getty Images/ iStockphoto/ Thinkstock, Getty Images/ Hemera/ Thinkstock

Squid

Page 126: Getty Images/ iStockphoto/ Thinkstock
Page 127: Alexandramp/ Dreamstime
Page 128: Jupiter Images/ Photos.com/ Getty Images/ Thinkstock, Hemera/ Getty Images/ Thinkstock, Getty Images/ iStockphoto/ Thinkstock
Page 129: Comstock Images/ Getty Images/ Thinkstock, Peter Leahy/ Bigstock
Page 130: Getty Images/ iStockphoto/ Thinkstock
Page 131: Getty Images/ iStockphoto/ Thinkstock, Getty Images/ iStockphoto/ Thinkstock

Turtles

Page 132: Getty Images/ iStockphoto/ Thinkstock, Hemera/ Getty Images/ Thinkstock, Jupiter Images/ Photos.com/ Getty Images/ Thinkstock, Getty Images/ iStockphoto/ Thinkstock
Page 133: Getty Images/ iStockphoto/ Thinkstock
Page 134: Getty Images/ iStockphoto/ Thinkstock
Page 135: Hemera/ Getty Images/ Thinkstock
Page 136: Image Village/ Dreamstime
Page 137: Getty Images/ iStockphoto/ Thinkstock
Page 138: Michael Humling/ Bigstock
Page 139: Rinusbaak/ Dreamstime
Page 140: Getty Images/ iStockphoto/ Thinkstock, Getty Images/ iStockphoto/ Thinkstock
Page 141: Getty Images/ iStockphoto/ Thinkstock, Getty Images/ iStockphoto/ Thinkstock
Page 142: Getty Images/ iStockphoto/ Thinkstock
Page 143: Getty Images/ iStockphoto/ Thinkstock, Getty Images/ iStockphoto/ Thinkstock

Whales

Page 144: Hemera/ Getty Images/ Thinkstock, Fuse/ Getty Images/ Thinkstock, Fuse/ Getty Images/ Thinkstock/ Getty Images/ iStock-photo/ Thinkstock
Page 145: Camp Crazy Photography/ Bigstock
Page 146: Getty Images/ iStockphoto/ Thinkstock
Page 147: Robert Raimo/ Bigstock
Page 148: Camp Crazy Photography/ Bigstock
Page 149: Corey Ford/ Bigstock
Page 150: Joanne Westen/ Bigstock
Page 151: Getty Images/ iStockphoto/ Thinkstock
Page 152: Getty Images/ iStockphoto/ Thinkstock, Getty Images/ iStockphoto/ Thinkstock
Page 153: Getty Images/ iStockphoto/ Thinkstock/ Volare/ Bigstock
Page 154: Design Pics RF, Getty Images/ Thinkstock
Page 155: Getty Images/ iStockphoto/ Thinkstock/ Hemera/ Getty Images/ Thinkstock

Sources

1. Axolotl
TORAH TALK — adapted from the *Aram Soba Newsletter, Parashat Ki Tesse* 5761, posted on the Shema Yisrael Torah Network, www.shemayisrael.com.

2. Coral
TORAH TALK — adapted from the *Aram Soba Newsletter, Parashat Toldot* 5759, posted on the Shema Yisrael Torah Network, www.shemayisrael.com.

3. Crocodile
WET, WILD, & WONDROUS — adapted from "Noah's Ark," a feature of chabad.org. *To learn more about Judaism and animals, visit www.chabad.org/NoahsArk.*
TORAH TALK — adapted from *Ohr Somayach Institutions*, which used the following sources: *Abarbanel Commentary to the Torah / Shemos* 7:28 / *Tehillim* 105:30 / *Tehillim* 78:45 / Rashi, *Shemos* 8:17, citing *Midrash Tanchuma*.
Some material was also adapted from "Noah's Ark," a feature of chabad.org. *To learn more about Judaism and animals, visit www.chabad.org/NoahsArk.*

4. Dolphin
TORAH TALK — Message (not the parable) was adapted from *Pirkei Avos* 4:1.

5. Duck
TORAH TALK — adapted from an article written by Rabbi Label Lam, with permission from *Project Genesis - Torah.org* (where a version of it first appeared).

6. Eel
TORAH TALK — adapted from *We Are Not Alone*, written by Rabbi Adi Cohen and published by Maagaley Yosher Institution.

7. Elephant Seal
TORAH TALK — adapted from the *Aram Soba Newsletter, Parashat Korach 5760,* posted on the Shema Yisrael Torah Network, www.shemayisrael.com.

8. Frogs
WET, WILD, & WONDROUS — adapted from "Noah's Ark," a feature of chabad.org. *To learn more about Judaism and animals, visit www.chabad.org/NoahsArk.*
"A Peaceful Ending" — adapted from *The Animal Kingdom in Jewish Thought*, by Shlomo Pesach Toperoff. Published by Jason Aronson Publishers, Inc. Jason Aronson is an imprint of Rowman & Littlefield Publishers, Inc.
TORAH TALK — adapted from an article written by Rabbi Naftali Reich, with permission from *Project Genesis - Torah.org* (where a version of it first appeared).

9. Jellyfish
TORAH TALK — adapted from an article titled, "Everything I Need to Know I Learned from a Jellyfish," by Rabbi Moshe Katz and Rabbi Doni Deutsch of the Chicago Torah Network.

10. Manta Ray
TORAH TALK — adapted from the *Aram Soba Newsletter, Parashat Pinchas* 5760, posted on the Shema Yisrael Torah Network, www.shemayisrael.com.

11. Octopus
TORAH TALK — adapted from the *Aram Soba Newsletter, Parashat Shemos* 5759, posted on the Shema Yisrael Torah Network, www.shemayisrael.com.

12. Penguins
TORAH TALK — adapted from an article titled, "Penguin Encounter," from zootorah.com.

13. Piranha
TORAH TALK — adapted from an article titled, "Something Fishy," by Chevrah Lomdei Mishnah/The Society for Mishnah Study, with permission granted by founder and president, Rabbi Moshe Haikins.

14. Seahorse
TORAH TALK — adapted from the *Aram Soba Newsletter, Parashat Chaye Sarah* 5759, posted on the Shema Yisrael Torah Network, www.shemayisrael.com.

15. Sea Otter
TORAH TALK — adapted from the *Aram Soba Newsletter, Parashat Nasso* 5760, posted on the Shema Yisrael Torah Network, www.shemayisrael.com.

16. Sharks
TORAH TALK — adapted from the *Aram Soba Newsletter, Parashat Tetzave* 5764, posted on the Shema Yisrael Torah Network, www.shemayisrael.com.

17. Snail
TORAH TALK — adapted from an article written by Baruch Sterman.

18. Squid
TORAH TALK — adapted from the *Aram Soba Newsletter, Shabbat Chol Hamoed* 5762, posted on the Shema Yisrael Torah Network, www.shemayisrael.com.

19. Turtles
TURTLE INTRODUCTION — portions adapted from "Noah's Ark," a feature of Chabad.org. *To learn more about Judaism and animals, visit www.chabad.org/NoahsArk.*
WET, WILD, & WONDROUS — portions adapted from "Noah's Ark," a feature of Chabad.org. *To learn more about Judaism and animals, visit www.chabad.org/NoahsArk.*
TORAH TALK — adapted from an article written by Rabbi Dovid Rosenfeld, with permission from *Project Genesis - Torah.org* (where a version of it first appeared). Some material was also adapted from "Noah's Ark," a feature of Chabad.org. *To learn more about Judaism and animals, visit www.chabad.org/NoahsArk.*

20. Whales
TORAH TALK — adapted from an article written by Rabbi Naftali Reich, with permission granted from *Project Genesis - Torah.org* (where a version of it first appeared).

* Secular information was obtained in part by the online animal encyclopedia — www.a-z-animals.com.

** Except for quoted factual data, the contents of secular websites named as sources are not endorsed by the Author or the Publisher.

If you love animals, and want to marvel at Hashem's creation,
this book is for you!
The Jewish WORLD of WONDERS PRESENTS:
Exploring the Wild World of ANIMALS
Marvels of Creation from a Torah Perspective
Efraim Harari
Exploring the Wild World of ANIMALS
A colorful safari featuring 35 beautiful and unique animals!
Israel Bookshop Publications
A must-have for children, teens, and adults!